Wembury Coastline and The Great Mew Stone South Devon

Arthur L. Clamp

The sentinel-like square tower of St. Werburgh's Church overlooks the beach and much of the coastline. It acted as a beacon years ago to mariners sailing close to the shallow waters.

This version of the book is virtually as originally published.
There are now additional pages at the back providing information about the author.

The republishing project is being managed by Arthur's grandson, Steven Gibson. We aim to find all the research that he was involved in publishing, preserving it for the next generation as part of 'The Clamp Collection'.

INTRODUCTION

It is hoped that this illustrated booklet will help in answering some, at least, of the many questions posed by visitors about the island and the general places of interest along this attractive coastline.

The South Devon coast is a beautiful combination of cliffs, valleys, estuaries with other features which make a visit to any of its areas interesting and rewarding. Large stretches of it can be easily covered by the determined walker and access through Devon's many small roads by the motorist is not too difficult.

The south-west corner of the county is bounded by an almost dramatic coastline made up of high, rugged cliffs and scenic estuaries. Wembury's coastline easily matches the attraction of other lengths and is bounded by the narrow Yealm estuary and the rocky foreshore of the eastern side of Plymouth Sound. It is enhanced by St. Werburgh's Church breaking the line of the coast and, of course, rightly claims to have one of the two largest islands off South Devon just over a mile from its rocky shore.

The island, attractive coastline and the steep sides of the Yealm estuary make this small area one of almost outstanding beauty combined with a rich heritage of maritime activities.

Wembury Bay and foreshore has been declared a marine conservation area (see appropriate page) as its shore and sea life are of particular richness and variety not normally encountered within such a small area.

This booklet has been divided into sections on the island, shipwrecks, walks, etc., and the visitor should have no trouble in identifying the various places of interest through its numerous illustrations. It is finally hoped that its use will help people to find and appreciate these features and the booklet be a pleasant reminder of visiting this part of the large county of Devon.

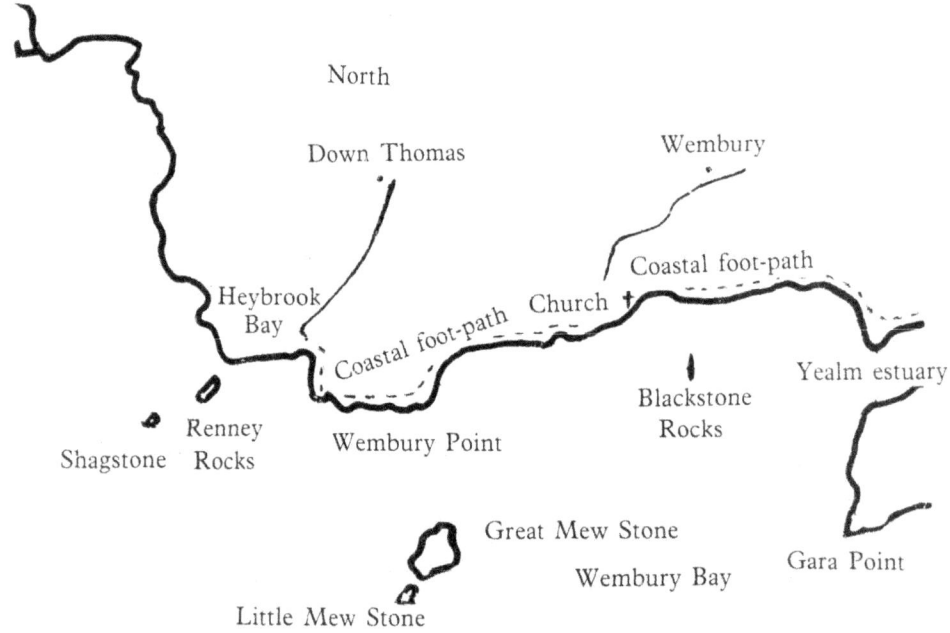

THE GREAT MEW STONE

This small conical-shaped rocky island stands about three-quarters of a mile from Wembury Point and is the largest offshore islet for many miles along the South Devon coast. Its name is an old English word for the common gull and rightly describes it as the home of this bird as well as many others, numerous plants and, for some years, one or two families. It appears that it was part of the mainland many years ago and, as recently as the 1800s, people could wade over to it at low tide. This is no longer possible. On its seaward side is Little Mew Stone and also on that part of the island stands the remains of a small building believed to be the home of the Wakeham family during the second quarter of the last century. The island was part of the Langdon Court Estate lands up until 1928 when it passed into a private individual's ownership (see article).

THE MEW STONE

Islands always appear to fascinate people especially if they cannot normally be reached or if information about them is sparse and inconclusive. The Mew Stone is such an island well within viewing distance yet few people manage to reach it because of the currents swirling between it and Wembury Point and the hazards of landing and leaving it at various stages of the tides.

Visitors to this area are always very curious about it and want to know if anyone is living there or what has happened on it over the years. The truth of the matter is that there is very little conclusive evidence to say what precisely has taken place on it apart from the unfortunate ships which have floundered on its rocks. These details can be read under the shipwreck section of this booklet.

It is known that it was part of the Langdon Court Estate for many hundreds of years until a change came in 1928 and, in subsequent years, various owners, it was reported, had different intentions of either using it as a summer residence or to cultivate its slopes. Nothing came of these ideas and the island still stands as it has done so for the past 200 years or more.

Tradition says that a local man was banished to it in 1744, guilty of some misdemeanour and confined to the island for seven years. He lived on it with his family and when allowed to return his daughter, known as *Black Joan*, declined to leave. She later married, had three children on the island, and only left when her husband was drowned in its turbulent waters.

In the early 1800s the island became the home of Samuel Wakeham and his wife Ann. He altered an existing building on it, prepared a small area for a garden and kept poultry and a couple of pigs. Seaweed and sand was used to manure the garden.

He held the land rent free from C. Calmady, Esq., of Langdon Court, with the right to eat anything that grew upon it on condition that he protected the island's rabbits out of shooting season. A local magazine of the 1830s tells at some length about Sam Wakeham's character and how he would welcome visitors from Plymouth who hired boats to bring them out for the day. For the benefit of the day trippers he erected a flagstaff on the island, cut steps for the ladies and *hewed out of solid rock a pair of thrones, wherein the lover of nature may sit and indulge his solitary musings.*

In 1834 it is recorded that he wrote, *If any Gentlemen what likes a wark, he can wark to the shoar at Wembury, and if they holds up there white pocket-handerchiefs for a signal, an ile cum off in me bote and fetch them to the island for two pence a pease, theres a bewtiful landing place dead eastered on the island an sum stairs that I made to cum up for the ladeys, an ile be very much oblige to put this in your booke you maid a mistake I be not forty ears old I be only 39 and 6 months.*

Sam might have lived out his life on this small island but records say that he engaged in smuggling activities and he was lured into a trap by a local excise man. Finally it was written, *Sam Wakeham has abdicated his throne on the Mewstone and is about to retire into private life by plying as a boatman of the Barbican Steps.*

So brings to an end speculation about one or two of the island's inhabitants. The local parish records tell a slightly different story. An entry in the Newton Ferrer's church register reads: *1778 Fynn, George, son of John and . . . at the Mewstone.* From the Wembury church register reads: *Burials, 1720 April 22 Lydia Sampson and John Sampson, 23, William Lee, 28, William Blatchford. May 15 Richard Cragg, Robert Sampson, Mary Avent, Mary Hake, John Tingcomb, 17, Josias Avent, 21, Walter Avent, 29, Mary Beer, 30, Elizabeth Taylor. Drowned between the Mew Stone and the Continent on a Sunday.*

The island is left as home for many gulls and other birds without rabbits or men to despoil its fragile covering of plants and soil. Only on the seaward-facing side can be seen the remains of a small round building and the word "private" chiselled in to a nearby rock.

SAM WAKEHAM'S DWELLING

This close view shows the stone dwelling when it was in a fairly good condition with a small extension behind it. The island is seen here at low tide from the very rocky foreshore.

The sea-bird claims that solitary spot,
The *Mewstone*; and around loud screaming wheels
In undisturbed possession. Other sounds,
Save those of shrieking winds, and battling cliffs,
Are seldom heard in that deserted isle!
The spirit of desolation seems to dwell
Within it; and although the sun is high,
And nature is at holy peace, it has
An aspect wild and dreary. Even now
The waves are rudely breaking at its base,
And a white feathery girdle clasps it round.
But in the wintry storm, when all that sea,
The terrible Atlantic, breasts its rocks
In thundering conflict, the unearthly howl
Might almost wake the dead!
               But here, are scenes,
Which if the wildness of the seaward view
Has giv'n the mind a melancholy tone,
Will yield a sure relief. 'Tis but to turn,
And all the landward view unfolds itself;
Soft flowing streams, and harbours wide, and towers,
Fair seated villages, and peace-crown'd cots,
And noble Mansions mantled deep in woods,
With all the humbler leafage springing up
From those warm hedge-rows that make England seem
A region of fair gardens. There the Yealm
Strays murmuring among his wooded cliffs;
And on his banks is *Langdon*, seated deep
In its own clust'ring groves, and who would hope
Who haply treads that desert bay below
Where ends the course of Yealm, to find so near
A spot so sweet as *Langdon*. Fairer scenes
Than those that lie beneath the raptur'd eye
This green isle knows not: ever varied too
Is the full prospect; valleys softly sink
And uplands swell, no level sameness tires,
While in the distance, happily dispos'd,
Sweeps round the bold blue moor.

ISLAND REPORTS

These two newspaper articles tell of changes of ownership for the island and new plans for its use but these, to date, have not taken place. The above poem, dated 1823, tells of the writer's feeling about the views and island as seen from an "elevated position" near Langdon Court. The description of the area has not really changed at all, the wind still blows and the shrieks of sea birds can be heard at most times of the year.

THE MEWSTONE

MANY people find the impulse to own an island quite irresistible.

When Mr. R. A. Stansell, of Heybrook Bay, intimated that he wished to dispose of the precipitous and unfertile Mewstone one imagined that there would be no great demand. But the contrary happened. All sorts of people in need of an island came forward without delay, and Mr. Stansell who bought the Mewstone in 1927 for £500 has found a customer, a Miss Goldman, of London, at £575. Some of the would-be purchasers expressed the intention of using the rock as an island retreat, where they could commune peacefully with the south-west winds and the seagulls, but the new owner is evidently fonder of ordinary society and is only to use it at week-ends.

The Mewstone is not the most delectable of islands, being small and Gibraltar-like in aspect, but at all events it is an island. Possession means the possession of a compact kingdom and the sensation which Alexander Selkirk experienced—though in larger degree—of being "lord of the fowl and the brute." There are island-owners scattered all around our shores and they apparently find their hobby most exhilarating.

SUMMER ON THE MEWSTONE

OWNER RENOVATES ANCIENT BUILDING

It is understood that Mr. John Goldman, the owner of the Mewstone, at the mouth of the River Yealm, intends to inhabit the island at some time during the summer.

The old stone hut on the island is being renovated. This is a round building with a stone roof and granite doorway, so old that there is no record of its age. Together with a lean-to shed adjoining it, it affords the only protection against the weather.

Residents at Wembury and Heybrook Bay are showing great interest in the activities. Mr. Goldman has been staying recently at Newton Ferrers and visiting the island by boat.

The Mewstone was given him as a wedding present by his sister, Miss Hazel Goldman, when he married the Hon. Margaret Thesiger, youngest daughter of the Dowager Viscountess Chelmsford, three years ago. The island formerly belonged to Mr. R. Stansell, of Heybrook Bay, who sold it for £575.

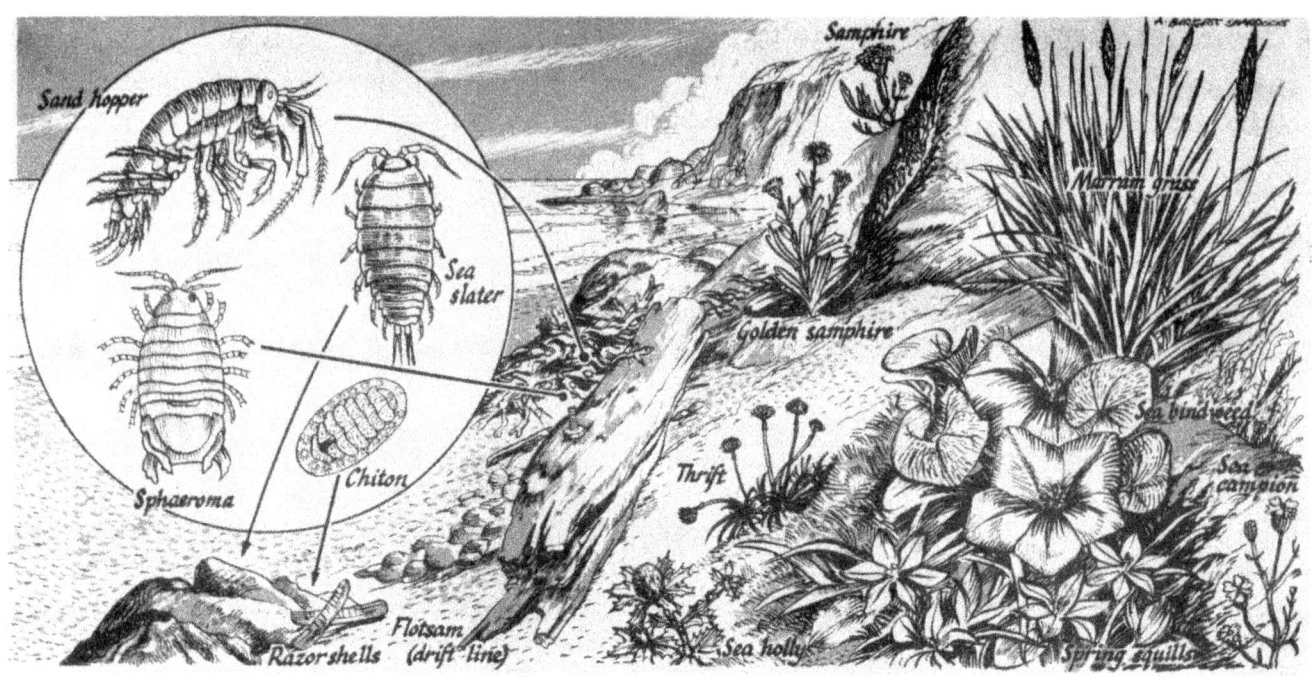

WEMBURY MARINE CONSERVATION AREA

The coastline between Plymouth Sound and the Yealm estuary and the shallow waters offshore have been declared a marine conservation area because of the variety and richness of plant and animal life on the shore and in the water. The variety of shoreline from rocks to small pebble and sandy beaches and the flow of water into the sea from the Yealm and various rivers into the Sound, have combined to produce an almost unspoilt habitat for sea creatures and shore plants of interest to visitors and students alike.

There is no restriction on access to the beaches or for exploring the numerous rocks and pools but visitors and residents are advised not to take away any examples of sea creatures and not to deliberately damage plants however insignificant they may look. It is hoped that this careful restraint will enable many visitors to look, observe or photograph things they see for many years to come. The pools, rock crevices and ledges are home to many thousands of living plants and creatures and it is this safe habitat with abundance of food from the sea which has given rise to this area being one of exceptional marine interest.

There are one or two small locally produced leaflets which explain quite adequately for most people the range of seashore life which can be seen at various levels of the tide. They are well illustrated. The Nature Conservancy Council in its leaflet, *The Seashore and You*, takes the interest a stage further while Collins produces an excellent illustrated book for anyone wanting to make a study of shoreline marine life.

These two drawings show some aspects of the variety of life to be found along the Wembury coastline at different levels of the beach and shallow water. They are useful in introducing people to the subject. Whatever is one's interest in this subject, care should be taken over not destroying habitats by leaving stones turned over or cutting seaweed from crevices and allowing the sun to dry out normally wet or damp rocks harbouring creatures waiting for the next tide.

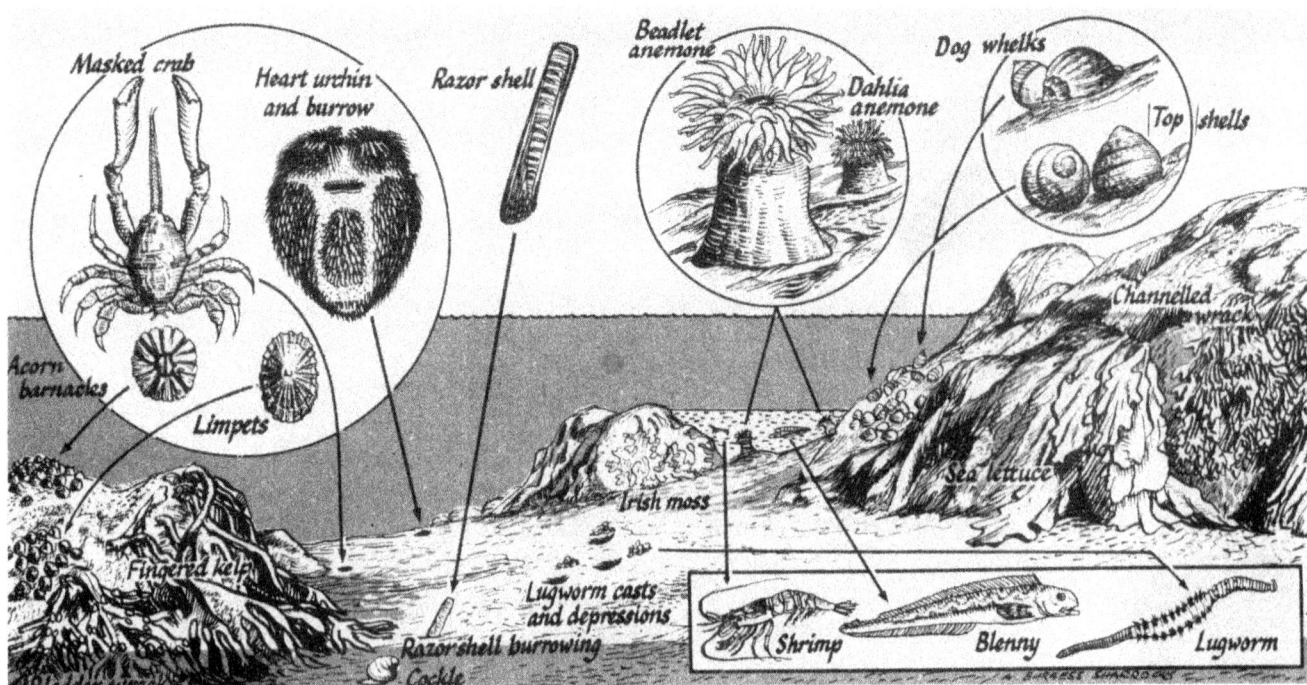

SHIPWRECKS IN THE AREA

The Wembury coastline from the Yealm estuary to the dangerous Shagstone Rocks, butting out into one of the main shipping lanes into Plymouth, and the presence of the Great and Little Mew Stone islands have presented many hazards to shipping making for or leaving the safe port of Plymouth, especially under bad weather conditions.

A quick look at the map will show that this coastline forms the eastern headlands to the Sound matched by those at Penlee Point and other places on the Western or Cornish side of the Sound.

Shipping, sail or steam, would have to enter the eastern or western channels at either end of the Breakwater and so be compelled to come in rather close to the shoreline. This was normally not a difficult course to steer and pilot cutters would be on duty outside the Breakwater to bring in large vessels unfamiliar with Plymouth waters. However, in spite of navigation charts, buoys and permanent landmarks, risks were often undertaken by moving vessels across these waters in bad weather conditions or without checking courses and positions with sometimes the inevitable tragic results.

The large island and rocky coastline have claimed their own when negligence occurred and the records show a steady number of small and large ships floundering for a variety of reasons.

This coastline, being near a large port, has had more than its fair share of wrecks and many of these are still lying where they broke up. The area has attracted many divers and from time to time artefacts are brought up, some of which are now kept in the nearby large Fort Bovisand.

There are many other remains on the seabed which indicate the presence of unrecorded wrecks. The following is a brief description of the known wrecks and how some of them came to grief.

Jeune Adelle: A small vessel which was wrecked on the Great Mew Stone during a storm in December, 1814.

John: She went aground on the Blackstone Rocks in November, 1824, and is remembered through the gallantry shown by James Cragg, a Yealm boatman, who was posted to guard over the wreck. In spite of the strong wind and the boat being 100 yards or more out in the water, he suddenly saw some movement on the wreck and immediately swam out through the strong waves to find the body of the captain's wife who was unconscious. He tied her to himself and swam back to the shore where helping hands soon relieved him of the heavy body. His very brave rescue was marked by an award from the Royal National Institution. It is thought that a grave to Thomas Willis in St. Werburgh's comes from this wreck.

Industry: This small Jersey owned smack came to grief on the Great Mew Stone during a gale on 16th January, 1851.

Ocean Queen: Tragedy occurred for most of her crew when this 206 ton brig from London hit the Little Mew Stone on 26th December, 1852. She was laden with general cargo and only one of her crew of fifteen was saved from the waters swirling around this outcrop of rock. She was a total loss.

S.S. Ajax: This steamship was built in Liverpool in 1843 for the Cork Steamship Company and served the Cork to London passage often calling at Plymouth en route. She was 206 feet in length, weighed 800 tons and was carrying 350 passengers with a general cargo when she hit the Great Mew Stone at about 5 p.m. on Friday, 13th October, 1854. Despite panic amongst the passengers no souls were lost and the passengers were taken back to Plymouth by boats from the Dockyard assisted by H.M.S. *Calcutta*. No satisfactory explanation has been given why this large vessel should be steaming so close to the shore. She was valued at £60,000 with cargo and eventually became a total loss and much of her is still in position not too far below the waterline.

Matilda: This was a small fishing vessel which hit the engines of the S.S. *Ajax* which lay awash. The wreck occurred on 1st March, 1866, and was tragic in that only the boy, William Bunce, was saved from a crew of three.

Western Star: She was wrecked at some point between Wembury Beach and the Yealm estuary on 1st January, 1873. She was a Bideford schooner of 74 tons and was built in Appledore in 1869. While on passage from Zante to Plymouth, close to the Eddystone, and in fog, her captain, Silvanus Williams, called to the skipper of a passing trawler about directions for Plymouth. He was given incorrect information and eventually came close to land, wrongly identifying Gara Point at Rame Head. He turned about but it was too late and he hit the shoreline rocks.

S. S. Rothesay: This is another large vessel to meet its end on the Great Mew Stone, this time close to the old dwelling on the island into which the passengers sought shelter. It sank on 15th October, 1854, and was a 332 ton coasting vessel carrying cargo from Caen to Cardiff. She was a total wreck. Having called in at Dartmouth for bunkering, her captain unwisely took to sea in a gale and was soon at the mercy of a force eleven gale. Captain G. Nance decided to make for the safety of Plymouth and as she approached waves pushed the ship onto the Mew Stone rocks. Her bottom was quickly torn apart and the captain had no choice but to abandon the vessel and wait for rescue on the wind-swept sides of the small island.

The Constance: She was lost on the Shagstone on 21st January, 1888, in thick fog while en route from Antwerp to Bristol with a general cargo. In spite of the fog the captain increased the engine revolutions to full speed at 3.30 a.m. The vessel safely passed the Mew Stone and seemed set to enter Plymouth Sound. Some of the crew were, in fact, on the forecastle preparing the starboard anchor in readiness to anchor once inside the breakwater, when the carpenter saw breakers ahead and shouted, "Captain, for God's sake port your helm." He reacted almost at once but to no avail. The *Constance* hit the inside of the *Shagstone* bows on and the hull, riding up over the ridge of rocks, ripping her bottom out open as she continued to move forward.

Baroda: This was a most unexpected shipwreck. She had been following in the wake of the S.S. *Nepaull*, less than 100 yards clear of the large steamer, when she grounded on the Shagstone and became a total loss.

There are, doubtless, many more wrecks lying in this area but the passing of time has left them unrecorded. References to three more wrecks help to fill in the picture. These are *The Brothers*, wrecked on Wembury Beach in 1854, the *Friends*, wrecked in 1852 between the beach and the Yealm, and a brig named *Jane* wrecked on the Mew Stone in 1804.

S.S. NEPAUL

The steamship *Nepaul* was wrecked on the Shagstone Rocks in December, 1890, en route to Plymouth from Calcutta having disembarked most of her passengers at Marseilles. She is one of the largest ships to come to grief in the Plymouth area, being 375 feet long and had a weight of 3,536 tons. She could carry 160 passengers, the mail and considerable cargo.

It was customary for pilots to wait outside the Breakwater to guide visiting ships into port but on this occasion the captain decided to enter the Sound without help as the pilot cutter could not be seen in the prevailing foggy conditions. He mistook the light of a small trawler for that of the cutter and quickly hit the Shagstone tearing away her forefoot. Distress rockets were sent up and the pilot cutter came to the rescue landing eleven passengers at Millbay.

No lives were lost but the very large vessel was considerably damaged and it was hoped to float her off the next high tide. This did not happen and she was declared a total loss.

S.S. VECTIS

This two-masted steamer of 907 tons was wrecked in February, 1912, on rocks near Andurn Point and was broken up during the great Christmas hurricane of that year.

Owned by John Hill of Sunderland she had unloaded her cargo of coal in the Cattewater and had put to sea en route to Cardiff in ballast. For some unknown reason the captain's mate altered the set course and before anything could be done she ran over the jagged rocks at this small headland. The crew were rescued by the Plymouth lifeboat and taken to the Barbican and it was thought that she could be refloated easily on the coming high tide.

She was stuck fast on the rocks and although the first mate remained on board for some weeks, it was eventually realised she could not be freed. The very strong gales of the winter soon broke her up and made her a complete wreck.

BREAKWATER PINNACE DISASTER

This stone records part of the tragedy which occurred on 7th November, 1838, when three pinnaces left the Breakwater for the Cattewater carrying men working out there. One of them capsized in the Sound and twenty men were drowned casting gloom over the town and leaving forty-nine children fatherless. The men mainly came from the Oreston area but William Cornish was of this parish. A public subscription was opened for the widows and orphans and many churches preached on the calamity the following Sunday.

RELICS FROM THE SEABED

This photograph of a small collection of bottles and stoneware jars is just a fraction of the many items that are brought up from year to year by divers exploring the area for shipwrecks, looking for objects or even fishing off the bottom or in the underwater rocks. The many ships which have gone down along this coastline must have carried thousands of interesting objects many of which are now covered with mud or sand and will probably never see the light of day. Occasionally large or interesting things are brought up such as cannon, anchors, etc. and sometimes a rare object will be discovered of which little is known. A few years ago a very old astrolobe was found, a navigating instrument of a simple kind to locate a ship's position.

RENNY ROCKS

The very dangerous rocks of hard quartzite are exposed for an hour or two each side of low tide and terminate with the solitary Shagstone which have claimed ships coming in too close to the shore when entering or leaving the safe anchorage of Plymouth Sound. Visitors are not advised to venture out to them; they are better viewed from the nearby low cliff.

WEMBURY CHURCH

This mainly fifteenth century church stands well away from Wembury village occupying a prominent position close to the rocky foreshore and overlooking much of Wembury Bay. There was most likely a Saxon wooden building here in the first place followed by a stone Norman church and then the present building, all of which have acted as beacons to nearby shipping as well as meeting the normal spiritual needs of parishioners.

The dedication is uncommon and is to St. Werburgh, daughter of the first christian King of Mercia who reigned from 659 to 675. Although isolated for many years, the area has been developed of late and the church has links with Australia, the Lords of the Manor and its graveyard contains stones recording shipwrecks and accidents in and around Wembury Bay.

It is certainly worth visiting especially on a summer's day as part of a general visit to the area or a break in one of the various walks along this attractive coastline. Spend a moment or two in its graveyard — a lot can be gleaned here about the perils of the sea and who were the locally important people years ago. The general appearance of the building shows that it has been weatherbeaten for countless years and now looks mellow with age. Buy the small guide booklet, this will tell you much about the history of the church and the area and list the different outstanding monuments inside whose links go out in many directions.

The interior was altered during the 1880s as part of the restoration scheme and this is much of the present interior as seen today. Use the guide booklet and a very pleasant and rewarding hour can be spent here where worship has taken place for many hundreds of years.

The Hele Memorial showing Sir John and Lady Hele with their youngest son to the right.

The oldest part of the church, the Norman south porch, is overshadowed by the later square tower.

An interesting feature is seen here, the original cobbled floor and large studded door.

Gravestones can tell much about local matters and here this interesting one recalls the passing of an old servant of Rear Admiral Charles Calmady.

The west-facing door of the church. Fifteenth century and a little worn with age.

THE OLD MILL

The present National Trust buildings were part of the ancient parish mill which ground corn and other products for Wembury farmers. This early photograph shows the *launder* which carried the gushing water down to the large overshot wheel providing the turning power for the large granite stones rotating in the building. Farmers brought their corn here and later returned to collect the flour for sale or bread making. The mill fell into disuse during the 1890s and remained derelict for some years until being converted into the existing building.

The cafe and other facilities usefully serve the many local and holiday people who come to this beach. Read the list of local people on page sixteen to see who was working the old mill.

The varied nature of the rocky coastline and small beach provide many opportunities for children and parents to explore the pools and exposed rocks for all kinds of interesting shore animals and plants. Good footwear should be worn as the rocks can easily cut the feet and slippery surfaces often cause people to fall.

HEYBROOK BAY AND H.M.S. CAMBRIDGE

The residential Heybrook Bay locality nestles in a small valley running down to the rocky foreshore between Renney Rocks and the headland now occupied by H.M.S. *Cambridge*. It can be reached via Down Thomas and grew from a small number of houses on the low cliff edge built during the inter-war years. It has a public house, the *Eddystone Inn*, but no shops. Later housing has taken place on the higher ground. The very dangerous Shagstone and Renney Rocks jut out some way into the sea where shipping must come in fairly close to sail or steam between the Breakwater and Staddon Point to reach safe anchorage in Plymouth Sound.

H.M.S. *Cambridge*, a Royal Naval gunnery school, occupied a holiday camp site on the headland at the outbreak of the last World War and since then has extended its training facilities for personnel. Between 1950 and 1972 permanent quarters were built and modern training facilities developed for practice firing over the sea. The colourful wooden figurehead of H.M.S. *Sphynx*, 1846-1881, stands at the entrance to the school although it is not known what connection it has with the old gunnery ships. H.M.S. *Cambridge* was commissioned in 1956 when other training facilities were moved here to form one large establishment.

WALKS ALONG THE COAST

Another very pleasant walk can be had by following the coastal path towards Plymouth as far as Heybrook Bay just out of sight beyond H.M.S. *Cambridge*. It runs along the edge of the low cliff as far as Wembury Point facing the Mew Stone and, at low tide, numerous rocks break the water's surface between the Point and the island showing how both were part of the same land mass many years ago. Part of an old boat house can be seen here which had its origins in the days when a local boatman could be called upon to take visitors over to the island. This is no longer possible.

The path skirts the naval training school which will display red warning flags when firing practice is taking place but this does not normally occur during weekends or at holiday times. The path climbs up overlooking the small Heybrook Bay on the far side of which is the dreaded Renny Rocks and the Shagstone jutting into the eastern approach shipping lane to Plymouth Sound. The path continues beyond this hamlet to Bovisand and the whole length is part of the very long coastal foot-path of South Devon.

The return to Wembury car park can be made back along the same route affording different views over the foreshore but another way is to take the narrow path up to H.M.S. *Cambridge*, a rather steep climb, then through part of this naval establishment out towards Spring Road. Turn right at the road and this will bring you partway back towards the houses close to Wembury Point from where a short path descends down to the coast path. Wembury will then only be about half a mile to the east.

Wembury Parish Council produce an excellent little booklet giving details of many walks with a large plan of the area. If visitors are staying in the locality this is well worth buying as many of the suggested walks criss-cross the parish linking the various hamlets and villages together. The generally high land will give good views over the sea and inland where Dartmoor forms a high blackcloth to the Devon landscape.

WALKS ALONG THE COAST

The large car park below the church at Wembury beach is a very good place for exploring the coastline although, it must be pointed out, in summer it soon gets full. A walk down from the village to the beach will, however, give walkers an excellent view of the Mew Stone and the church on the left.

There is a good foot-path running round to the River Yealm which can easily be followed from the car park. The path climbs above the level of the church, which should be visited, then follows the high cliff towards the isolated New Barton Farm. It descends down to Season Point, at the mouth of the Yealm facing Mouthstone Point on the opposite headland, then continues down to Warren Point which faces Noss Mayo.

The National Trust notice advises visitors about keeping dogs on a lead as grazing animals are allowed along this area to keep the scrub under control. Rocket Cottage will be passed before the path descends down towards the estuary passing some mature fir trees which form a frame to the view of the Mew Stone when seen higher up the estuary.

The villages of Noss Mayo and Newton Ferrers flank either side of the small creek running off from the main Yealm estuary and the area has become well known for its scenic beauty and private yachting. The

last stretch of foot-path brings into a view an excellent panorama of the villages with woodlands covering much of the shoreline land. The path finishes at Warrent Point where a small boat crosses the creek and, further along, the private notice brings to an end this walk some yards from the old coastguard cottages.

The return walk to Wembury can be varied by following the path up the steps to Rocket Cottage then along the track to Monkswood and Wembury House. The road or path can be followed back to the car park but it is advisable to carry a map for this length or make use of the foot-path map of the area from the Post Office.

MAJOR EDMOND LOCKYER AND AUSTRALIA

The Australian flag in St. Werburgh's Church was presented by the Government of Western Australia in 1941 to commemorate the establishment of the first British Colony in Western Australia in 1826 by Major E. Lockyer whose family had been in residence in Wembury House. The present building was built by his father, Thomas, 1803 to 1806.

Edmond Lockyer had a long and distinguished military career. On instructions from the Governor he arrived at King George Sound on Christmas Day, 1826, with a detachment of troops and prisoners on board the *Amity*. He landed on Boxing Day and raised the British flag on 21st January, 1827, followed by a royal salute, claiming Western Australia for the crown. Only then did the whole continent come under the British flag. The settlement was later called Albany.

This Plymouth son whose family made such a mark on the town and who prospered through trade, buying the Wembury estate and building the present fine house, continued the long tradition of exploration and colonisation engaged in by Drake, Hawkins and many others.

TWO INTERESTING BUILDINGS

The above dated building stands about half a mile from Wembury Beach and Rocket Cottage, below, near Warren Point, tells a story in its title linked with calling out local coastguards when a shipwreck occurred.

Wembury

Is a village and parish 5½ miles south-east from Plymouth, in Plympton St. Mary union, in the deanery and hundred of Plympton, in the Parliamentary division of Totnes, archdeaconry of Totnes, diocese of Exeter, South Devonshire, on the sea coast, overlooking Plymouth Sound. The church of St. Werburgh is a small edifice, and the living, a vicarage, is in the gift of the Deans and Canons of Windsor. The pop. in 1881 was 551; in 1891, 572.

POST & TELEGRAPH OFFICE—Jas. Drake, postmaster. Letters arr. at 7.45 a.m. and 4.45 p.m.; desp. at 9.40 a.m. and 5.45 p.m. Sundays 10.0 p.m.

BOARD SCHOOL—Wm. L. Scarr, master Mrs. Scarr, mistress

PRIVATE RESIDENTS.
Burgess Rev C. vicar
Clay Dr. Wembury house
Cory Richard J.P. South Wembury house

COMMERCIAL.
Beer Wm. farmer, Wembury mill and farm
Catte Benjamin, junr. farmer, Old Barton
Cocks Ernest, farmer, Radleigh farm, Down Thomas
Coleman Jno. blacksmith, Knighton
Coleman Nicholas, farmer, Spurwell
Drake Jas. postmaster
Edwards E. farmer, Manor farm
Giles Herbert, farmer, Page's farm
Hurrell Thos. *New inn*, Down Thomas
Mildren Daniel, carrier and general shop
Mitchell J. general shop
Nelder Arthur, farmer, New Barton
Pearce Harold, farmer, Langdon Barton
Perrin Alfred, *Jubilee inn*, Knighton
Pursley Wm. farmer, West Wembury
Scarr Wm. Lord, schoolmaster
Spurrell Wm. farmer, Down Thomas
Symons J. blacksmith, Down Thomas
Tolchard Elias, wheelwright, Down Thomas
Williams Richd. farmer, Gabber farm
Wilson James, farmer, Traine
Wilson John P. Princes farm

WEMBURY, 1900

The above article shows who was living in Wembury at the turn of the century and gives some information about the parish when it was well in the country and quite undeveloped as a residential area.

Rogation Service at St. Werburgh's Church

This open air service is thought to date around 1950 and held during the three days before Ascension Day often in May. The weather is good for this occasion and the backdrop of the sea ideal.

Going back to Willowhayes field after Milking

A once familiar sight in Ford Road when Mr. Godfrey Smallridge brought his cows back from milking at West Wembury Farm. The year is 1952, the house *West Wembury Cottage*, and the cows Friesians and Ayrshires.

1913: The Bryant family on Wembury Beach

Joseph, Mary, his wife, and their son Jack lived in the old mill and they occasionally allowed visitors in for tea and the use of their musical box for 1d. The family soon left for New Zealand after this photograph was taken where they set up a new home.

We have combined two publications in one book. Modern publication methods mean that the very short books produced by Arthur L Clamp need to be combined with others in order to reach minumum page numbers. The cover photos of 'Recollections of Wembury' are included above to ensure that there is a complete record in this publication. The second book follows.

Recollections of

WEMBURY

Arthur L. Clamp

The Old Mill at Wembury Beach

This pre-1914 photograph records what the working corn mill looked like with its large over shot wheel and wooden launder down which the water flowed. The wheel was probably scrapped for metal during the First World War; the mill ceased working around 1900 and the miller was a Mr. William Beer.

INTRODUCTION

This illustrated booklet recalls much of Wembury and its people during the years 1900 to 1960, a half century of time when enormous changes took place in almost all walks of life. The physical make up of the area has also changed from a farming community to a residential community its people now working mostly away from the village and land in the Plymouth area.

This booklet is a record of those days in which everyone knew everyone; there was a clear social structure up to the landed gentry with Langdon Court being the main residence and land ownership largely in the hands of a few families. The period is marked by two world wars with many local people losing their lives in action, a population change from about 500 to now between 3 to 4,000 people with radical changes in forms of transport allowing individuals to move around the greater Plymouth area with ease and speed undreamt of before the coming of the car.

The world no longer finishes at the county border. Through radio, television, and the cinema a thousand images can be thrown on screens in almost all homes in the parish opening the mind to places, people and events hitherto unreached.

On a more practical level homes now have electricity, gas, running water, flushed toilets or at least soak-aways. The cutting of firewood, delivery of coal and the street seller of all kinds of domestic items has been replaced by going to the superstores at Plymstock or over to Lee Mill.

The horses have gone, farming methods changed and now very few are employed on the land. The hedge trimmers have gone, the daily delivery of milk by horse and cart a thing of the past. Yes, these years have seen great changes. It is very appropriate that a record be made, however inadequate, of scenes once common to Wembury that will linger on in the minds of readers of local books.

Acknowledgements and thanks are recorded here to many local persons for their help in a variety of ways. Robert Rowland, Fred Rowland, Doris Harvey, the late Miss Eileen Drake, Mrs. Fone, Mr. and Mrs. B. Butler, Mr. G. Smallridge, Miss M. Bojanitz and others come readily to mind. Also encouragement from members of the Wembury History Society with Dick Thorpe at their head, must be included. This booklet is dedicated to all the local people of Wembury parish who have contributed to the heritage of these acres in a corner of the county of Devon.

Arthur L. Clamp,
203 Elburton Road,
Plymouth, Devon.
1995

Knighton Telegraph Office

Was this the first post office in the Wembury locality? "Rose Villa" is seen here around the turn of the century and the man is given as James Drake, holding the watering can, with "Floss" next to him. Did this scene predate the scene at Watergate when Knighton Post Office was there (see page 10). Note the letterbox set in the window. Inset: Is this Miss M. Perring?

ESTATE OFFICE,
LANGDON COURT,
PLYMSTOCK.

March 3rd 1899

William Drake was with me for Five Years and during that time, I always found him Honest, Sober, Steady & Industrious, he is one I can thoroughly recommend

W. J. Sherwill
Clerk of Works.

Confirmation Dress
It was a common practice for young lady candidates to be specially dressed for confirmation. Edna Sly poses for the photographer for her confirmation at St. Werburgh's Church in 1938. Charles Young was then the vicar.

Mr. and Mrs. A. Dixon
This 1920s studio photograph was taken when Mrs. Annie Dixon was school mistress at Wembury school. They were then living in the old school house; it is not known what her husband did for a living.

At the Warren
This car was parked here sometime in 1928 making a good background to Georgie, Edna and Lily Sly who were out for a walk along the coastline. Lily was later to become a monitor teacher at Wembury School.

Farm Sale Catalogue 1947

Farms change hands from time to time and this title page from the sale of New Barton farm recalls such an event. It passed from Mr. A. Nelder to Mr. J. Partridge being made up of 196 acres of arable land, 70 acres of pasture land and 2 acres of homestead and garden. There was then stabling for 6 horses, a shippen for 20 cattle and an engine house for a pumping plant. Calves and pigs houses were also listed to which a "useful wartime air raid shelter" was added.

Particulars

AND

Plan and Conditions of Sale

OF THE

Freehold Mixed Farm

KNOWN AS

NEW BARTON

WEMBURY, South Devon

TELEPHONE No. WEMBURY 218

TO BE SOLD BY PUBLIC AUCTION AT THE

Law Chambers, Princess Square, Plymouth

ON

Thursday, 21st August, 1947, at 4 p.m.

With Full Vacant Possession on Completion

Auctioneers:
PETER HAMLEY & SONS,
11 Princess Square,
Plymouth.
Telegrams: Auctioneers, Plymouth.

Solicitors:
WHITEFORD, BENNETT & WOOLLAND,
2 North Hill Place,
Plymouth.
Telephone: 5045 Plymouth.

Langdon Boat House

The top of this solitary building at Wembury Point is seen beyond the stooks of corn sometime in the very early years of this century. In 1881 it is recorded that James Hockaday, aged 32, boatman, his wife Harriett, 33, and Raymond, 1, a son, lived here. Later the Axworthy family came with many children. A living was made by catching fish and shellfish and, presumably, rowing occasionally to the island.

Off to the Fields

It is about 1956, the month is August, and Fred Rowland and Bob Penwill supervise the collection of sacks of barley left by the combine harvester in fields at Traine farm. Jackie, Susan and Robert Rowland, Angela and Roger Grant with Adrian Pate and Keith Fretsome, have been identified.

Shipwreck at Wembury

This occurred on 18th November, 1895, when the *August Smith*, a Norwegian barque carring 1,500 tons of logwood was bound for Rotterdam from Buenos Aires. Seaweed is being collected from the beach probably used as compost for potato crops.

Billiard and Ballroom

Built in the early years of this century at South Wembury House the rooms allowed many social functions to take place here. The Cory family had daughters and provided opportunities for gatherings among the well off in those days.

Wembury Mill 1895

The *August Smith* lies without rudder which was broken away in a gale causing her to drift on to the rocks. All the Norwegian crew were rescued. The close view of the mill shows the launder down which the leat water ran to operate the overshot water wheel. William Beer was given as farmer and miller at this date.

Ice Cream at the Farm

Yes, this could be bought at West Wembury Farm for just 3d. with cream as well! Bertha Steer, Phyllis Steer, Aunt Flo, Edna and Lily Sly are enjoying themselves during a summer in the late 1920s. As they were dressed with hats it must have been a special occasion.

Wartime Wedding

Family and friends are gathered around George Harris and Lily Sly at Hollacombe House. They had just been married at St. Werburgh's Church on 20th June, 1942, when the groom had home leave for this special occasion.

Star Motor Bus

Wembury, Heybrook Bay and Down Thomas had a bus service into Plymouth run by J. W. Newton and Sons from 1923 to 1959. This Morris bus did service in the 1930s seen here with Mary Taylor. The luggage could be carried on the roof access to which was up the iron ladder.

Char-a-banc Outing to Exmouth

Violet Cars run by Mr. A. E. K. Rodgman, Pomphlett, hired out this pneumatic tyre open tourer to the villagers of Wembury seen here on 30th August, 1924. William Drake with his wife Eliza have been recognised. It was quite common for these open coaches to take people away for a day's outing when the majority of people did not have cars and there were few buses.

Miss E. Drake and her Motor Cycles

In order to get to her schools at Oreston and later at Sparkwell Eileen Drake became a familiar figure in the area riding a variety of motor cycles and later cars. Here she is on 26th June, 1929, on a B.S.A. 250, no. JY 5127, and the insurance certificate is shown as well. She also had a Francis Barnett, DR 8765 (1932), Francis Barnett YY 1111 (1935), and a Coventry Eagle CCO 953 (1943) before going on to drive cars.

ROAD TRAFFIC ACTS, 1930 to 1934, Y 50.
AND
MOTOR VEHICLES & ROAD TRAFFIC ACTS (NORTHERN IRELAND), 1930 to 1934.

Certificate of Insurance.

Certificate No. 548868.
1. Index Mark and Registration Number of Vehicle: J.Y.5127. BSA 250
2. Name of Policy Holder: Miss E.L.Drake.
3. Effective date of the Commencement of Insurance for the purposes of the Act: 5th February 1935
4. Date of Expiry of Insurance: 29th November 1935.
5. Persons or Classes of Persons entitled to drive*
The Policyholder.
The Policyholder may also drive a Motor Cycle not belonging to him and not hired to him under a hire purchase agreement.
Provided that he holds a licence to drive the vehicle or has held and is not disqualified for holding or obtaining such a licence.

Cycling around Wembury

The year is 1928 and Lily Sly and her cousin Dorothy are off for a ride from Hollacombe House around Wembury. The occasion was remembered as one bicycle was borrowed from Eileen Drake.

A Royal Visitor to Wembury

King Edward VII and Queen Alexandra at Langdon Court on a shoot of some kind between 1902 and 1907. With them are General Way, Admiral Bouverie Clark, Mrs. Bessie Cory, Colonel George Gone and Admiral Sir Alexander Buller with others. The staff are dressed for the visit showing the coachman, butlers and two chefs. There must have been quite close links between the owners of Langdon Court, the Corys, and royalty for this visit to have taken place.

John Henry H. Smallridge

He worked with his father at West Wembury Farm and is photographed here in June, 1951.

Raking up the Hay

Mrs. Muriel Smallridge is seen here with *Rocket* the farm horse at West Wembury Farm for about twenty years. It is in the late 1940s, the month is June for hay racking. The horse is remembered as being playful and inclined to kick out.

West Wembury Farmer

John Henry Smallridge took over this farm in 1931 from Mr. and Mrs. Pursley and worked it until the late 1970s. He is here holding his grandson, Harry; he came from Brixton.

Punch and Rocket Farm Horses

These were returned each day to their pastures down Ford Road as seen here sometime in the early 1950s. Mr. John Smallridge normally had three horses working on his farm in the village.

Watergate

Miss Minnie Perring ran Wembury post office from the first of the four cottages at Watergate from about 1908. Soldiers in the First World War sent letters from home and one, a Mr. Brown, later married her and ran the office after 1918. A shop was also ran for a time by Mr. and Mrs. Walke from the last cottage.

A Last Farewell

This family group was recorded on 11th June, 1913, on Wembury Beach showing Joseph, Agnes and Mary Bryant who later emigrated to New Zealand. The occasion is not known but from their clothes it must have been an important one accompanied by their dog.

Post Office and Telegraph Office

A closer view is given here of the first cottage at Watergate ran as a post office by Alfred Perrings in 1890 followed by James Drake in 1899, 1903, then Miss Minnie Perring, 1910, changing to Mrs. Minnie Brown up to 1926 and possibly later. The office was transferred to the Square.

Wembury House
Built in 1803 by Thomas Lockyer on the site of an earlier building this view dates from the early years of this century when it was occupied by Dr. Robert Hogarth Clay, M.D. who followed Ralph Dawson as its owner.

James Walke
He is seen here as the full time gardener at Langdon Court succeeding his father in this work when he died. Mr. J. Walke was a local builder before this undertaking a variety of jobs around Wembury.

Wembury House Lodge
Many large country houses had an entrance lodge in which estate families lived. John Northcott, coachman to Mr. Ralph Dawson who then lived in Wembury House, was here in the 1880s with Thomas Sansome and his son Edmond then given as gamekeepers. A horse and trap was at times later taken to Plymouth to collect Dr. Clay from his practice in Plymouth.

The Jubilee Inn, Wembury

Known now as the *Odd Wheel* Inn, it was run by Alfred Perring who was here from at least from 1899 until at least 1926. Prior to him was Mrs. Ann Collier and before Nicholas Coleman was given as an innkeeper and blacksmith with his wife Georgina. The photo probably dates from the late 1920s as electricity had not yet been laid to the village or inn.

Wembury Dance Band

This was formed during the war years in the early 1940s for dances in Wembury on Saturday evenings held in the old village hall, an ex-Army hut replaced in 1956. Formed by Clem Spencer it also shows Terry Griffin, Fred O'Connor and Barbara Mitchell at the piano.

Carol Service at the Jubilee Inn (now the Odd Wheel)

It is the 1950s and the Rev. Ken Tagg promoted this occasion for some years during Miss Lottie Perrings time at the inn. Muriel Woods, Harold Willcocks, Bert Woods, Alice Butler, Patsy Somerville, Doug Butler, Dianna McDonald, Don McDonald, Olive Harvey and Mrs. Willcocks make up this festive group.

Wembury

Is a village and parish 5½ miles south-east from Plymouth, in Plympton St. Mary union, in the deanery and hundred of Plympton, in the Parliamentary division of Totnes, archdeaconry of Totnes, diocese of Exeter, South Devonshire, on the sea coast, overlooking Plymouth Sound. The church of St. Werburgh is a small edifice, and the living, a vicarage, is in the gift of the Deans and Canons of Windsor. The pop. in 1881 was 551; in 1891, 572.

COMMERCIAL.

Beer Wm. farmer, Wembury mill and farm
Cane Benjamin, junr. farmer, Old Barton
Cook Ernest, farmer, Down Thomas
Coleman Jno. blacksmith, Knighton
Coleman Nicholas, farmer, Spurwell

POST & TELEGRAPH OFFICE—Jas. Drake, postmaster. Letters arr. at 7-45 a.m. and 4.15 p.m.; desp. at 9.40 a.m. and 5.45 p.m. Sundays 10.0 p.m.
BOARD SCHOOL—Wm. L. Scarr, master; Mrs. Scarr, mistress

PRIVATE RESIDENTS.

Burgess Rev C. vicar
Clay Dr. Wembury house
Cory Richard J.P. South Wembury house

Down Thos. *New inn*
Drake Jas. postmaster
Edwards E. farmer, Manor farm
Giles Herbert, farmer, Page's farm
Mildren Daniel, carrier and general shop
Mitchell J. general shop
Nelder Arthur, farmer, New Barton
Pearce Harold, farmer, Langdon Barton

Perrin Alfred, *Jubilee inn*, Knighton
Pursley Wm. farmer, West Wembury
Scarr Wm. Lord, schoolmaster
Spurrell Wm. farmer
Symons J. blacksmith, Down Thomas
Tolchard Elias, wheelwright, Down Thomas
Williams Richd. farmer,
Wilson James, farmer, Traine
Wilson John P. Princes farm

1899

Burgess Rev. Chas. [vicar], Wembury cot
Calmady Miss, Knighton villa
Coleman Nicholas, Spurwell
Cory Richard J.P. Langdon court
Rodney Frederick, Bovisand lodge

COMMERCIAL.

Beer Wm. miller (water), Wembury mill
Cane Joseph, farmer, Knighton
Cannon Fredk. farmer, Wembury Barton
Coleman John, smith, Knighton

Coleman Nicholas, *Jubilee inn*, Knighton, & farmer, Spurwell
Giles Herbert Pitts, frmr. Down Thomas
Hurrell Servington, New inn
Lakeman Nicholas, farmer, Manor farm
Lang Frank, frmr. Train frm. Knighton
Nelder Thomas, farmer. Down Thomas
Pearse Thomas, farmer, Langdon Barton
Perring Alfred, postmaster, Knighton
Pote Robt. shoe ma. & sexton of the parish

Pursley Wm. farmer, West Wembury frm
Sherwill William, carpenter, Gabber
Spurrell William, farmer, New barn
Stevens John, farmer, Down Thomas
Symons John, blacksmith, Down Thomas
Tolcher Elias, wheelwright & smith, Down Thomas
Williams Richd. farmer, Gabber farm
Wilson Jas. frmr. Langdon Home farm

WEMBURY.

Burgess Rev. Charles (vicar), Wembury cottage
Clay Robt. Hogarth M.D. Wembury ho
Rodney Frederick, Bovisand lodge
Beer Wm. miller (water), Wembury mll
Clay Robert Hogarth M.D., L.R.C.S. Edin. surgeon, Wembury house
Cock Ernest, farmer, Down Thomas
Coleman Nicholas, farmer, Spurwell

Edwards William, farmer, Manor farm
Giles Herbt. Pitts, frmr. Down Thomas
Hurrell Thomas, New inn
Milden Daniel, carrier
Pearse Harold William, farmer & overseer, Langdon Barton
Pursley Wm. frmr. West Wembury fm
Sherwill Wm. farmer, Knighton farm
Spurrell William, farmer & overseer, Down Thomas

Symons Jn. blacksmith, Down Thomas
Williams Richd. farmer, Gabber frm
Wilson James, farmer, Traine farm
Wilson John, farmer, Down Thomas

KNIGHTON.

Coleman John, smith
Nelder Arthur, farmer, Newbarton
Parsons John, farmer, Oldbarton
Perring Alfred, Jubilee inn

PRIVATE RESIDENTS.

Peto Rev. John Frederick B.A. (incumbent), Welcombe house

COMMERCIAL.

Box William, farmer, Mead
Burrow Elijah, farmer, Tredown
Burrow Thomas, farmer, Linton
Cook James, farmer, Mead
Cornish Willie, carpenter

Cottle John, farmer, Lanapark
Dennis William, farmer, Leddon
Hedden William, yeoman, Upcott
Hockin William, farmer, Underhill
Howard Jesse Westlake, miller (water), West mill
Jeffrey John, farmer, Darracott
Metherell Ernest, farmer, Mead
Oke Edward, farmer, Well farm

Oke John, farmer, Upcott
Oke Samuel, farmer, East town
Oke William Jn. apartments, Strawberry Water
Oliver James, farmer, Henneford
Wade Richard, carpenter
Wakely Caleb, blacksmith, Darracott
Ward John (Mrs.) & Son, frmrs. Barton
Ward John, farmer, Henneford

WEMBURY is a parish on the south coast, 6 miles south-east from Plymouth, in the Tavistock division of the county, hundred of Plympton, petty sessional division of Ermington and Plympton, union of Plympton St. Mary, county court district of Plymouth, rural deanery of Plympton, archdeaconry of Plymouth and diocese of Exeter. The church of St. Werburg, situated close to the sea and at some distance from the village, is a plain building of local stone in the Early English style, consisting of chancel, nave, aisles, south porch and an embattled western tower containing 5 bells. In the church are several monuments, including one dated 1677 to the family of Calmady, and another on the north side of the chancel, and dated 1608, to Sir John Hele and his family: there are three parclose screens, erected from the designs of Messrs Hine and Odgers, architects, and executed by Hems, of Exeter; the ancient screen was taken down and destroyed about 1850: the church was restored and reseated in 1886 by the same architects, at a cost of £3,500, and affords 280 sittings. The register of baptisms and burials dates from the year 1611; marriages, 1612. The living is a perpetual curacy, net yearly value £566, in the gift of the Dean and Canons of Windsor, and held since 1923 by the Rev. Anyon Herbert Duxbury M.A. of Wadham College, Oxford. One of the ancestors of Vincent Calmady esq. in 1682 bequeathed £500, now £522 3s. 10d. Consols, to the parish, the interest of which is distributed in bread, coals and clothing. Langdon Court, a mile and a quarter distant, is the property and residence of Richard Wallis Cory esq. J.P. who is lord of the manor, which up to the time of the Dissolution belonged to the priory of Plympton; the house was built in 1577 by the families of Pollexfen and Calmady, and inhabited by them till 1875, when it was bought by Mr. Cory. It was rebuilt in 1707 by Josias Calmady. Wembury House was built by Sir John Hele, and was originally much larger than at present; it is occupied by Mrs. Cecil F. A. Walker. Thorn, the residence of the Hon. Mrs. Sebag-Montefiore, is a fine mansion overlooking the estuary of the Yealm. R. W. Cory esq. J.P. is the principal landowner. The soil is loamy; subsoil, clay and slate. The chief crops are wheat, oats, barley and turnips. The area is 3,131 acres of land, 2 of water, 30 of tidal water and 237 of foreshore; rateable value, £4,712; the population in 1921 was 501.

DOWN THOMAS, 1 mile north-west, and KNIGHTON, north-east, are hamlets. There is a Wesleyan chapel at Down Thomas.

Post, M. O., T. & T. E. D. Office, Knighton.—Mrs. Minnie Brown, sub-postmistress. Letters through Plymouth

Public Elementary School, built in 1876 at a cost of £734, for 80 children; Mrs. Annie Dixon, mistress

The school is controlled by six managers; Philip Bateman, Plymstock, correspondent

WEMBURY.

PRIVATE RESIDENTS.

(For TN's see general list of Private Residents at end of book.)

Case Rev. Joshua John, Boveysand lo
Cory Rd. Wallis J.P. Langdon court
Crohan Commdr. Patrick R.N. Bay cottage
Duxbury Rev. Anyon Herbert M.A. (vicar), Wembury cottage
Sebag-Montefiore Hon. Mrs. Robert, Thorn
Walker Mrs. Cecil F.A. Wembury ho

COMMERCIAL.

Marked thus † farm 150 acres or over.
†Andrews Lewis, farmer, Langdon Barton
Bridgman Martin, farmer, Traine frm
Cocks Ernest, farmer, Down Thomas
Dobson Herbt. View inn
Giles Herbert, farmer, Down Thomas
Giles Rt. Pitts, farmr. Down Thomas
Hoskin William, farmr. Gabber farm
Kingwell Jn. farmer, Manor farm
Milden Daniel, carrier
†Nelder Arth. R. farmer, New Barton. TN Plymstock 80X
†Pursley Bros. farmers, West Wembury farm

Reid Ernest Thos. farmer, Spirewell farm
†Sherwill Maurice Jn. farmer, Knighton farm
Slade Jn. farmer, Old Barton
Watts Geo. farmer, Ranleigh farm
Watts Wm. farmer, Langdown Home farm
Wilson James, farmer, Pages farm

KNIGHTON.

Rundle Col. George Richard Tyrrell C.B. The Cottage

COMMERCIAL.

Coleman John, smith
Perring Alfred, Jubilee inn

1926

Trade Directories

A record of what a community is made up of in its range of trades and businesses can be found in these books produced about every ten years from the 1860s. An interesting and valuable picture can be built up of the growth and changes that many villages go through including Wembury. The years shown here are for 1899, 1910 and 1926.

Loading the Hay Waggon

This 1942 group of local farm employees include Ken Wood, Bob Penwill, Ralph Avent, Doris Congdon, Sam and Bill Gibson, John Moses, Charlie Brook and Bert Wood. The horse, *Lion*, belongs to Fred Rowland of Traine Farm who is supervising the work. The hay would later be hand pitched to form a rick kept for cattle feed during the winter.

Early Car at Wembury

Miss Eileen Drake is at the wheel of her open Austin tourer taken about 1934. Her mother, and aunt Janet, are the passengers. She owned this car for about two years and was probably one of the first persons outside the gentry families, to run a car in the village. She exchanged this car for a motor cycle which she used for going to her school at Oreston. Petrol was obtainable from Folland's single pump and tank situated opposite the shops at the bottom of Knighton Hill.

Knighton Hill about 1903

None of the three persons in this very early photograph can be recognised showing a farm cart making its way past Four Corners and the stables. It is recorded that it was then occupied by a Mr. and Mrs. Crundell.

Milk Delivery to Plymstock

John H. Smallridge had to milk his cows, prepare for this daily milk round and be away from his farm in Wembury by 7 a.m. returning about 12 noon. He is here in Plymstock with Mrs. Treeby holding *Jess*. The round was about 14 miles and two 12 gallon milk churns were carried at the back of the cart.

Sunday School Scholars

One of the three girls is Violet Axworthy and they appeared on a postcard franked the year 1905. The former Wesleyan Methodist Chapel still stands as a private residence near Wembury House. Opened in 1871 it closed about 1913 and maybe because of its position was not a successful cause. It was recorded in 1881 that it had 91 seats.

Three Little Maids from the Knighton Wesleyan Sunday School

Langdon Court Gardeners

The two gardeners working in the 1920s were Jim Walke and G. Erstcott, head man. Like many other country seats Langdon had many staff for the house, grounds and the carriages for the family. Langdon estate was sold off in 1927.

BUNGALOID GROWTHS AT WEMBURY BAY

THREAT TO A LOVELY SEASIDE SCENE

ACTION BY PLYMPTON COUNCIL

WEMBURY BAY, BETWEEN THE mouth of the Yealm and Wembury Point, has always been considered to be one of the most beautiful stretches of coastline in Devon.

Now, however, it is in danger of being spoilt by the erection of variously-coloured wooden structures graced by the name of "bungalows," which clash hideously with the beauties of the landscape.

The spot chosen by the builders is the high ground behind the ancient parish church of St. Werburgh. This weather-beaten old church stands immediately above the foreshore. Overlooking it, a hundred yards or so away, are about a dozen of these "bungalows," which are used, apparently, by "week-enders" from Plymouth and elsewhere.

Some are quite roomy, and, though they certainly do not tone with the landscape, appear to be well built. But others do not! Greens and sickly pinks and reds on boards and corrugated iron, and old oil drums turned into water butts; the remains of a wooden shanty (which looks as though it might have been blown down in a gale) with broken glass lying around; old bus bodies, porched on concrete blocks; a railway carriage which has been converted into a habitation—these are features of the landscape.

If this sort of thing was allowed to continue, Wembury might soon become known as Shanty-town.

Bus body bungalows at Wembury Bay.

The Days before Planning Permission!

This November, 1932, newspaper article now makes interesting reading refering to the erection of various odd buildings above St. Werburgh's Church including the conversion of two very early Plymouth buses as weekend living quarters for Plymothians. The extent of this activity is not known but it may have died out by the time of the Second World War when the military authorities took over much of the coastline.

Wembury United Football Team 1951-52

Runners up in the Plymouth Combination League, Division 1 East, they played at the back of The Mount. Penny Horwell, Alice Butler, Barbara Scott, Ken Scott, Pete Lapthorn, Don McDonald, Des Deacon, Brian Sugden, Dave Lavers, Stan West, Lew Thomas, Dave Hurrell, Stan Cutchee, Jenny Spencer, Bert Spencer, Mar Butler, Arthur Ralphson, Clem Spencer, Roy Spencer, Brian Spencer, Roy Waterfield, Doug Butler, Gladys Cutchee, Diana McDonald and Elizabeth McDonald make up most of this group.

Mr. Dawson Wembury House	Rev. Richard Lane Minister	Coastguard
Mr. Dawson Wembury House	Mr. Coombe Langdon Farm	Mr. Tuckett Old Barton Farm
Mr. Calmady Langdon Court	Mr. Spurrell New Barton Farm	Mr. Tuckett Old Barton Farm
Mr. Calmady Langdon Court	Mr. Rider Train Farm	Mr. Caine Farm
Miss Calmady Knighton Cottage	Mr. Nelder Raneleigh Farm	Mrs. Horton Farm
Mr. Popplestone Down Thomas Farm	Mr. Lobb Farm	Mrs. Jackson Wembury Cottage
Farm Barton	Mr. John Wilson Farm	Servants of Wembury House
Mr. Lakeman Princess Farm	Mr. James Wilson Farm	Servants of South Wembury House
Mr. J. Williams Langdon House Farm	Mr. Nott Knighton Farm	Mr. Coleman Blacksmith
Servants of Langdon Court	Mr. and Mrs. Beer Wembury Mill	Mr. Collier Jubilee Inn

Seating Plan for St. Werburgh's Church in the 1870s

Box pews were almost universal in all churches many years ago and by making a charge or rent churches were able to gain an income from their use. In the case of Wembury the box pews as shown here were removed in 1886 and the present open seating plan pews installed. There were also 33 "free" seats in St. Werburgh's occupying other parts of the church.

Wembury School Children in 1928

The headmistress was then Mrs. Elizabeth Nicholas, on the right, assisted by Miss Florence Axworthy on the left. The children identified are Peter Gill, George Body, Edwin Milden, John Fansom, Pearl Roberts, Lilian Beer, Violet Badcock, Dora Body, George Walke, Jimmy Wills, Jimmy Rowe, Albert Newton, Dennis Goodman, Ian McClaren, Smith, Charlie Ford, Raymond Brown, Willy Ford, Edna Sly, Iris Walke, Ivy Newton, Polly Newman, Violet Andrews, Elaine Nichols, Alma Yatches, Arthur Yates, Frances Woodley, Clifford Walk, Winnie Walk, Tich Edgcumbe and Betty Brown.

A Meal Break at Harvest Time

The photograph dates from the early 1940s at Old Horn. The bungalow in the background is *The Nook* and the corn rick was being built just inside the hedge butting Church Road. In view are Bill Woods, Mrs. Waite(?), Bill Towill, Blanche Smallridge and Harry and Olive Smallridge.

Fox Shooting in the 1950s

Foxes were quite a menace over the years and shoots were organised to reduce their numbers as recorded in this catch. Tom Staddon, Stan Williams, Bill Mildren, Arch Mildren, Willy Jenkin, Albert West, Edward Jenkins, George Body, Jim Booth, Joe McBean, Freddie Rowlands, Desmond Rider, Sid Smith, Jim Baker, Joe Rowlands and Harry Booth make up most of this afternoon shooting party.

Winter Fox Shoot at Wembury

Up to forty people would sometimes meet for these winter shoots along the Wembury coastline beating the ground cover then shooting the fox as it ran out. January was the best time when local farmers had some spare time for this day event. Led by Fred Rowland these shoots went on for about ten years. Here one fox has been shot and looking on are Roy Harvey, Joe Rowland, Terry McCoy, Mr. West, Stan Williams and others.

Wembury Dock

A grand scheme for constructing a large dock along the foreshore at Wembury which would be linked to a railway was proposed in 1908 but nothing came of it. Known as the new Plymouth Ocean Harbour Scheme at Wembury Bay its backers were hoping to land passengers from transatlantic liners which were then becoming such a feature of Plymouth's waters.

The Wembury (Plymouth) Commercial Dock and Railway.

Blacksmith's Shop

This view of the bottom of Knighton Hill probably dates about 1910 when the smithy was the hub of the village and farming community in which dozens of horses worked and were shoed here. Closed about 1945 it was worked for many years by various members of the Coleman family among whom are remembered George, Nicholas and Jack, three brothers with John Coleman being recorded working here from at least 1870 to the 1920s.

Knighton Hill in the 1930s

An approximate date can be given for this later view as electric lights were then working, power coming to Wembury in 1937-8. The road and cottages look somewhat less rural than the earlier photograph.

Thatched Wembury Cottage

This still stands at the bottom of Knighton Hill but now has a galvanised roof. It was the home of Mr. and Mrs. Mildren at the time of this photograph and shows young Jimmy Mildren standing in the road.

Knighton Hill about 1920

Seen here as a country lane, Granny Avent and her daughter in law are in view alongside the cottages once occupied by Phyllis Avent, James and Jane Walke, Elizabeth Cawse, widow with two children. The field opposite belonged to Knighton Farm.

Gravestone Tribute

Many local people spent most of their working lives employed "in service" to gentry families. This record of James Seward, a servant of Rear Admiral C. Calmady of Langdon Court, is typical of past patterns of work although the majority have long gone with no record of their life long service.

Mr. and Mrs. J. Avent in 1927

They celebrated their diamond wedding on 2nd March, 1927, aged 82 (Joseph) and 83 years (Elizabeth). They had 7 children, 10 grand-children and 2 great grandchildren and they lived at Knighton for most of their lives.

```
           LANGDON COURT ESTATE,

              Nr. PLYMOUTH, DEVON.


Messrs. Fox & Sons in conjunction with Messrs.
Viner Carew & Co. beg to remind you of their
important Auction Sale of the above, to be
offered in a large number of lots, at the
Royal Hotel, Plymouth, on Thursday next, the
29th September, 1927, in two sessions at
11 a.m. and 2.30 p.m. precisely, when they
hope to be favoured with your attendance.

Auction Offices:  Bournemouth and Plymouth.
```

Sale Notice Reminder

This postcard reminded prospective buyers of the Langdon Court Estate Sale held in 1927. A Mrs. Kenyon-Slaney bought the house and ten acres of land and tenant farmers were able to purchase their own farms.

Going down to Wembury House

This early postcard view shows the buildings of Old Barton Farm, John Parson and later John Slade were given as farmers here in the 1910s and 1920s, and the tall chimney of the Lodge is also seen at the top of Thorn Drive. The card probably dates from the 1910s.

Wembury Almshouses

Built in 1662 at the expense of Sir Warwick Hele, these almshouses were erected for housing six local families. A chapel was incorporated in the long building in which daily readings were made for the residents.

Church Road in the 1940s

This solitary delivery van denotes the then small amount of traffic in the parish. To the left is Bay Cottage guest house then owned by Com. and Mrs. Clunch who are also remembered as always keeping bulldogs.

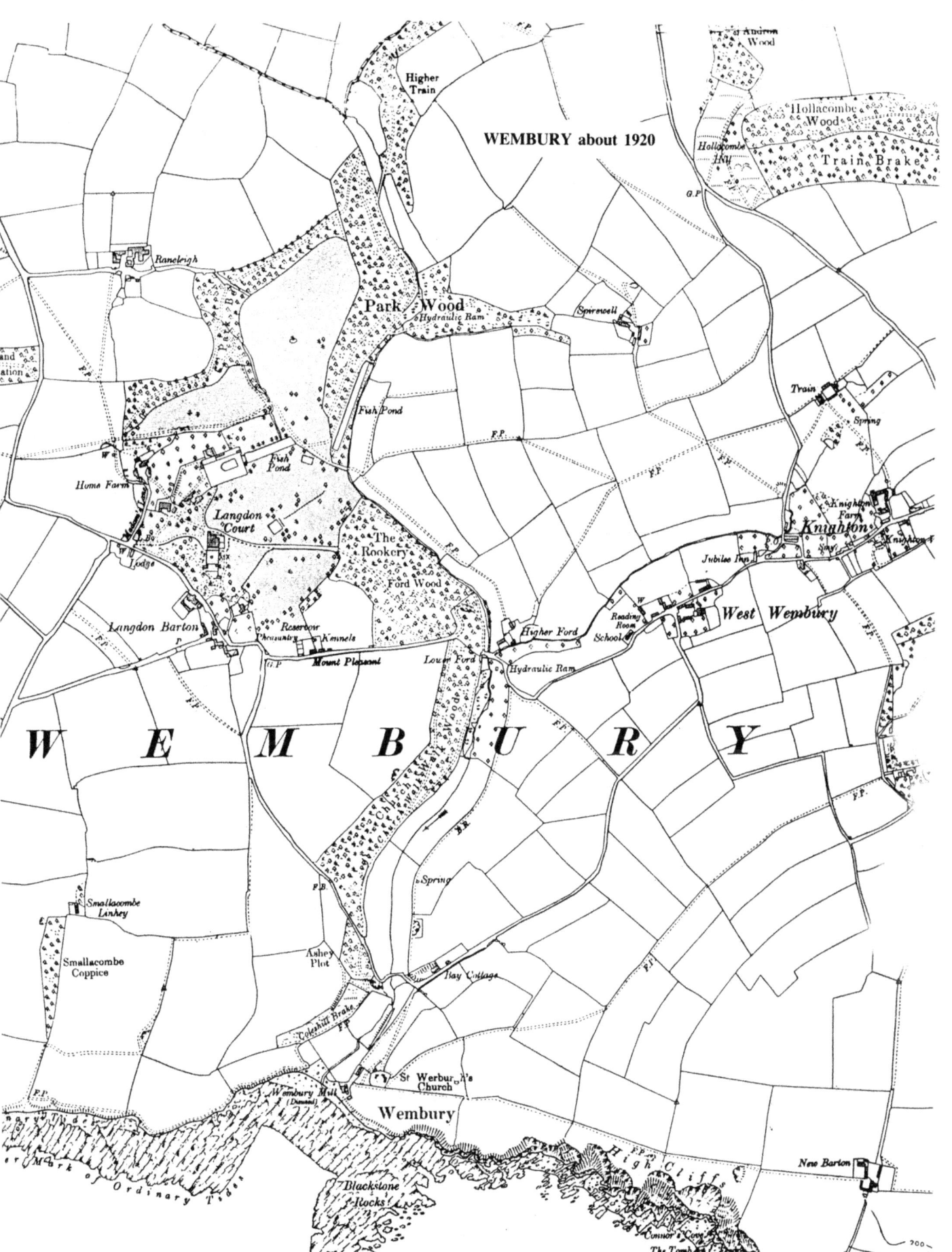

Wembury United Football Club, 1949-50

They were the cup winners for the Plymouth Combination League and they played next to Treefields. Recognised are Des Deacon, Dusty Millar, Alf Full, *hon. treas.*, Kenny Woods, Herb Spencer, Stan Cutchee, *hon. sec.*, Pete Lapthorne, George Fiern, Arthur Williams, Horace Horton, Stan West, George Bannaford, *hon. chairman*, Arthur Ralphson, Denny Horwell, Clem Spencer, Doug Butler and Roy Spencer.

A Day Outing starting from the Square, Wembury, in the 1940s

Mrs. W. Radmore organised these from time to time and on this occasion it is thought the coach is going to Paignton. George Radmore and Harold Hobbs shared the driving and many in the group have been recognised as Brian Perring, Brian Edwards, Alf Perring, Mrs. Pensam, Pop Rowe, Ida Rowe, Mrs. Willcocks, Mrs. Channing, Edna Hobbs, Verina Hobbs, Margaret Radmore, Beats Spencer, Francis Mildren, Winnie Radmore, Olive Harvey, Ronnie Weeks and Mrs. Stephens.

THE PEOPLE OF WEMBURY AS RECORDED IN 1881

All that part of Wembury which lies to the east of Wembury Mill leat including Spirewell Farm, Train House and Farm, Water Gate, and Ford Cottages, Wembury Mill and Cottage, New and Old Barton Farms, South Wembury House and Cottage, Coast Guard Station, Knighton Village and Farm, West Wembury Farm, Wembury Wood Cottage, Almshouses, Wembury House and Lodge and Hollecombe Lodge.

New Barton Farm
William Spurrell, Head of Family, 65, farmer, 280 acres, 2 men, 3 boys
Eleanor, wife, 75
William, son, 33
Jane, daughter in law, 30
William, grandson, 4
Elizabeth Wills, niece, 43
Robert Ellis, servant, 18
Robert Mildren, servant, 16
Thomas Rogers, servant, 15

Warren Cottage
Peter Lardeau, widower, 61

Coast Guard Station
John Segrue, Head of Family, 51, chief officer
Emma, wife, 39
Thomas Doble, visitor, 71

Coast Guard Station
Joseph Brown, Head of Family, 44
Matilda, wife, 44

Coast Guard Station
Charles Jago, Head of Family, 33
Emmaline, wife, 30
Emmaline, daughter, 3
Charles, son, 1

Coast Guard Station
James Barnett, Head of Family, 41
Elizabeth, wife, 48
Alfred, son, 10
Thomas, son, 6

Coast Guard Station
Edward Richards, Head of Family, 34
Mary, wife, 36
Edward, son, 6
Jenny, daughter, 3
Thomas, son, 1

South Wembury Cottage
Priscilla Blackler, Head of Family, 22, laundress
Rosina, sister, 17

Wembury House Lodge
Zachariah Bailey, Head of Family, 57, gardener
Martha, wife, 57, laundress
John, son, 18
William, son, 13

South Wembury House
William Ellis, Head of Family, 47, farm bailiff
Agnes, wife, 42

South Wembury Room over Stables
Agnes Squires, 80

South Wembury Lodge
William Harper, Head of Family, 41, gardener
Emma, wife, 41
Mary, daughter, 13, scholar
William son, 11, scholar
Francis, son, 9, scholar
Edwin, son, 7, scholar
Susan, daughter, 6, scholar
Helena, daughter, 5, scholar
Thomas, son, 3

Wembury Cottage
Henry Woolf, Head of Family, 39, mariner
Jane, wife, 40
Richard, son, 11, scholar
Frederick, son, 7, scholar
William, son, 6, scholar
Ernest, son, 4

Wembury Cottage
Thomas Weeks, Head of Family, 54, agricultural labourer
Susanna, wife, 46

Old Barton Farm
Frederick Cannon, Head of Family, 40, farmer, 163 acres, 1 man
Elizabeth, wife, 39
Frederick, son, 16
William, son, 12
Alfred, son, 7
Digby, son, 6
Ann Lane, 16, servant
Sophia Mumford, 11, servant

Wembury House
Ralph Dawson, Head of Family, 67, J.P. for Devon
June, wife, 62
Minnie, daughter, 22
Annie Crosby, visitor, 42
Ada Crosby, visitor, 20
Mary Anstey, 30, servant
Harriet Hoskin, 18, servant
Elizabeth Juda, 29, laundress
Mary Voysey, 19, cook
Jane Spurrell, 19, dairy maid

Wembury House Lodge
John Northcott, Head of Family, 58, coachman
Emma, wife, 49
Alice, daughter, 4, scholar

Almshouses
Charlotte Ware, Head of Family, 43
William Mitchell, Head of Family, 76
Mary, wife, 77
Sarah Ward, Head of Family, 67
Elizabeth Avery, Head of Family, 68
Patty Treblie, Head of Family, 73
Susanna Mildren, Head of Family, 74

Wembury Wood Cottage
Thomas Sansome, Head of Family, 55, gamekeeper
Amelia, wife, 50
Edmond, son, 16, gamekeeper
Mary, daughter, 13, scholar
Ida, daughter, 4, scholar
Thomas, son, 8, scholar

Cottage at Knighton
William Toms, Head of Family, 26, fisherman
Mary, wife, 26
Florence, daughter, 3
William, son, 1

Cottage at Knighton
James Mildren, Head of Family, 58, agricultural labourer
Jane, wife, 46
Daniel, son, 21, agri. labourer
Thomas, son, 13, scholar
James, son, 10, scholar
Elizabeth, daughter, 6 scholar
Henry, son, 8, scholar
Samuel, son, 2

Cottage at Knighton
Joseph Avent, Head of Family, 36, agricultural labourer
Elizabeth, wife, 38
Mary, daughter, 10, scholar
Emma, daughter, 8, scholar
Thomas, son, 6, scholar
William, son, 3

Cottage at Knighton
Andrew Walke, Head of Family, 57, agricultural labourer
Sarah, wife, 69

Cottage at Knighton
John Waters, Head of Family, 43, agricultural labourer
Mary, wife, 39, dressmaker
James, son, 10, scholar
Ellen, daughter, 8, scholar
Edwin, son, 6, scholar
Henry, son, 4, scholar
Emily, daughter, 2
Infant, 1 week

Cottage at Knighton
Joseph Algate, Head of Family, 68, agricultural labourer
Anne, wife, 50

Cottage at Knighton
Joseph Bryant, Head of Family, 59, agricultural labourer
Ann, wife, 60

Cottage at Knighton
James Walke, Head of Family, 39, agricultural labourer
Jane, wife, 42
Elizabeth, daughter, 15, scholar
Francis, son, 12, scholar
Emily, daughter, 10
James, son, 5
Sydney, son, 4
Alice, daughter, 5 months

Cottage at Knighton
William Algate, Head of Family,

The child in this picture is Iris Walke with her mother Amy Walke. They lived in the cottage below and the period is again the early 1920s.

Residents of Knighton Hill

The dresses almost give the period when this picture was taken in about 1912 showing Mrs. Jane Walke with her grand daughter, Lydia Cawse. Mrs. Emily Walke is on the outside, the three then living in this cottage.

Here standing in front of the same cottage (note the part slate-hung wall covering) is Elizabeth Cawse with her daughter in law, Edith Cawse, and the year is about 1922.

27, agricultural labourer
Elizabeth, wife, 26
William, son, 5
Charles, son, 3
Bessie, daughter, 1
Cottage at Knighton
Philip Cobley, Head of Family, 67, agricultural labourer
Jane, wife, 63
James, son, 32
Emma, daughter, 29
Adeline, daughter, 7
William, son, 6
Bertha, daughter, 4
Infant, 1 week
Cottage at Knighton
William Pitts, Head of Family, 46, agricultural labourer
Ann, wife, 39
Joseph Robers, son in law, 18, ag. labourer
James Roberts, son in law, 16, ag. labourer
John Roberts, son in law, 14, ag. labourer
Thomas Roberts, son in law, 12
Richard, son, 10
Priscilla, daughter, 7
William, son, 1
Elizabeth Avent, 77
Knighton Farm
Thomas Knott, Head of Family, 45, farmer, 145 acres, 3 men, 1 boy
Jane Brooking, 28, housekeeper
Priscilla Yabsley, 22, servant
Richard Mildren, 18, servant
Albert Algate, 15, servant
Cottage at Knighton
William Baddock, Head of Family, 56, thatcher
Anne, wife, 48
William, son, 23, wheelwright
Sydney, son, 21, invalid from Navy
Elizabeth, daughter, 13
Sarah, daughter, 13
Janet, daughter, 6
Charlie, son, 4
Beatrice, granddaughter, 3
Cottage at Knighton
Robert Jackman, Head of Family, 60, agricultural labourer
Elizabeth, wife, 60
Priscilla, daughter, 18
Amelia Rogers, visitor, 34
Caroline Rogers, visitor, 9
Florence Rogers, visitor, 5
Alice Rogers, visitor, 10 months
Cottage at Knighton
Lucy Blatchford, spinster, 26
Elizabeth Weeks, lodger, 17
Cottage at Knighton
William Weeks, Head of Family, 53, domestic gardener
Ann, wife, 44
James, son, 15, mason apprentice
Frederick, son, 8
Pheobe, daughter, 6

Henry, son, 12
Ernest, son, 4
Cottage at Knighton
Wiliam Beer, Head of Family, 33, farmer
Bessie, wife, 25
Wallace, son, 3
Cottage at Knighton
Alfred Perring, Head of Family, 26, painter
Maria, wife, 25
Cottage at Knighton
John Coleman, Head of Family, 70, blacksmith
John, son, 41, blacksmith
Mary, daughter in law, 31
John, grandson, 8, scholar
Nrash(?), son, 7
Matilda, daughter, 5
Ellen, daughter, 3
Nicholas, grandson, 11 months
Louisa Collier, 16, servant
Cottage at Knighton
Robert Wilmott, Head of Family, 30, agricultural labourer
Mary, wife, 33
Sarah, daughter, 10, scholar
John, son, 5
James, son, 2
Cottage at Knighton
John Webb, Head of Family, 60
Charity, wife, 65
Cottage at Watergate
James Drake, Head of Family, 39, groom, domestic servant
Ann, wife, 45
Anne, daughter, 14, scholar
Mary, daughter, 10, scholar
Lokiss(?), daughter, 8, scholar
Cottage at Watergate
William Walk, Head of Family, 61, carrier
Jan, wife, 60
Hart Body, son in law, 26, carpenter
Elizabeth Body, daughter in law, 24
Hart Body, grandson, 8 months
Cottage at Watergate
John Knox, Head of Family, 58, master mariner
Henrietta, daughter, dressmaker
Eva, daughter, 16
Philip Cobley, grandson, 4
Cottage at Watergate
Robert Pope, Head of Family, 65, shoemaker
Elizabeth, wife, 63
Anthony, son, 26, shoemaker
Emma Callard, granddaughter, 10, scholar
Cottage at Watergate
William Cobbledick, Head of Family, 77, Greenwich pensioner
Harriat, wife, 77
Cottage at Watergate
William Rogers, Head of Family,

48, agricultural labourer
Caroline, wife, 48
Caroline, daughter, 11, scholar
Cottage at Watergate
George Avent, Head of Family, 38, agricultural labourer
Ellen, wife, 36
Henry, son, 13
George, son, 11
Blanch, daughter, 7
Maud, daughter, 4
Train House
Francis Lang, Head of Family, 29, farmer, 145 acres, 2 men, 1 boy
Annie, wife, 28
William Budge, son in law, 40, servant
Henry Walke, 14, servant
Isabella Scantlebury, 24, servant
Cottage, West Wembury
Thomas Cawse, Head of Family, 30, agricultural labourer
Mary, wife, 31
Mary, daughter, 6, scholar
Robert, son, 6
Emily, daughter, 3
Cottage, West Wembury
John Rogers, Head of Family, 56, agricultural labourer
Elizabeth, daughter, 16
John, son, 12, scholar
William, son, 9, scholar
Elizabeth, daughter, 7, scholar
Cottage, West Wembury
Joseph Algate, Head of Family, 30, agricultural labourer
Sarah, wife, 39
Samuel, son, 4
Elizabeth Pitts, mother, 60
Cottage, West Wembury
William Algate, Head of Family, 42, general labourer
Jane, wife, 38
Ernest, son, 10, scholar
William, son, 14
Cottage, West Wembury
Thomas Algate, Head of Family, 42, agricultural labourer
Susanna, daughter, 15
William, son, 14, mason labourer
Mary, daughter, 9, scholar
Joseph, son, 8 scholar
Emily, daughter, 5, scholar
Richard, son, 3
West Wembury Farm
Edmond Knott, Head of Family, 56, farmer, 170 acres, 3 men, 1 boy
Solome, wife, 48
Ellen Lewis, 17, farm servant
William Eastley, 14, farm servant
Wembury Board School
Thomas Jordan, Head of Family, 68, pensioner from the Plymouth Breakwater, foreman over masons
Mary, wife, 54, teacher
Mary Lugg, 18, teacher

Wembury Stars Football Team in 1923

They were champions of the Plymouth and District League in 1923. Shown are Alf Brown (he ran the P.O.), Bill Griffiths, William Milded, Henry Milden, Jimmy Taylor, Clem Spencer, two Pedricks and four have not been identified.

Wembury Sports Trophies Awards in the 1920s

A low table of cups and plaques await presentation in front of the ex-First World War Army hut now in a somewhat dilapidated condition. To the left stand Mr. Tink and Joe Axworthy and, at the other end of the table, is Maurice Sherwell and Hildred Drake. A barrel organ and monkey were remembered being here for some entertainment.

Wembury A.F.C. in 1937-38

This team simply used a field for playing on and is now Ridge Cross playing fields. Recorded are Jimmy Rowe, *referee*, Nobby Andrews, Les Milden, Raymond Henshaw, Herb Spencer, Ned Harris, Albert Andrews, Eric Warley, Godfrey Milden, Raymond Brown, Albert Parsons. *Front row:* Len Stear, Bert Stear, Arthur Yates, Ben Hick and Roy Spencer.

Bay Cottage
William Sherrell, Head of Family, 25, carpenter
Martha, wife, 26
Sydney, son, 6 months

Wembury Mill
William Beer, Head of Family, 67, farmer, miller, 58 acres, 1 man
Bessie, daughter, 28

Hollicombe Lodge
Edmond Fowell, Head of Family, 58, civil service foreman of smiths
Mary, wife, 61

Jubilee Inn
Nicholas Coleman, Head of Family, 39, innkeeper and smith
Georgina, wife, 33

Jasper Collier, nephew, 21, smith app.
Flloyd Reid, 10, scholar
Alma Algate, 16, servant

Ford Cottages
Two uninhabited

Spirewell Farm
William Pursley, Head of Family, 34, farmer, 75 acres, 2 boys
Susan, wife, 28
Susannah, daughter, 6, scholar
Sophia, daughter, 3, scholar
William, son, 1
Samuel Axworthy, 20, farm servant
Francis Weeks, 14, farm servant
Maria James, 14, domestic servant
Samsin Johnson, 56, nurse
Daniel Cane, 80 ag. labourer

All that part of the parish of Wembury which lies to the west of Wembury Mill leat including Langdon Hall, Langdon Barton and Cottages, Ford and Gabber Villages, Gabber and Raneleigh Farms, Bovisand House and Cottages, Farm Barton, Down Thomas village and Princes Farm, Prins Farm, Leips Farm, Beers and Taylors Farm.

Langdon House
Richard Cory, Head of Family, 57, landowner
Julia, daughter, 28
Elizabeth, daughter, 23
George Yelland, 41, butler
Charles Andrews, 19, footman
Elizabeth Ryder, 26, ladies maid
Mary Goodchild, 35, house maid
Alice Mills, 30, kitchen maid

Langdon Stables
John Pattington, Head of Family, 26, groom
Henry Longthern, 21, groom
Joseph West, 20, groom

Langdon Lodge
William Pattington, Head of Family, 34, coachman
Charlotte, wife, 32
Helen, daughter, 4
Alice, daughter, 3
Evan, son, 2
Charles, son, 7 months

Langdon House Farm
John Williams, Head of Family, 63, farmer, 113 acres, 2 men, 1 boy
Mary, wife, 64
Sarah Parsons, daughter, 37
John Williams, grandson, 10, scholar
Kate Avery, niece, 24, visitor
John Blatchford, 16, servant

Raneleigh Farm
Thomas Nelder, Head of Family, 71, farmer, 400 acres, 4 men, 4 boys
Mary, wife, 60
Josias, daughter, 26
Lydia, daughter, 25
Mary, daughter, 21
Arthur, son, 19
Robert Slocombe, 17, servant
Cli Horn, 16, servant

Frank Simmons, 15, servant
John Budge, 13, servant

Bovisand House
Frederick Rodney, Head of Family, 59, gentleman
Phillipa, wife, 50
Evelyn, daughter, 23
Bertha, daughter, 16
Frances, daughter, 14
Henrietta, daughter, 13
Clementine, daughter, 12
Edward, son, 9
Reginald, son, 7
Elizabeth Williams, 20, cook
Mary Caunter, 20, house maid

Down Thomas Farm
Richard Popplestone, Head of Family, 81, farmer, 170 acres, 3 men, 2 boys
Mary, daughter, 54
Elizabeth, daughter, 47
Elizabeth Horton, niece, 42
Samuel Popplestone, 78, brother
Frank Doddridge, 20, servant
Sampson Hemmett, 17, servant
Emily Straw, 13, general servant

Cottage at Down Thomas
William Cobley, Head of Family, 37, labourer
Deborah, wife, 38
William, son, 13, scholar
Sarah, daughter, 11, scholar
George, son, 9, scholar
Mary, daughter, 6, scholar
Albert, son, 5, scholar
Ernest, son, 2
Sarah Watkins, 80

Cottage at Down Thomas
Matthias Avery, Head of Family, 33, shoemaker
Mary, wife, 38, dressmaker
Humphrey, son, 1

Cottage at Down Thomas
James Tall, Head of Family, 68, agricultural labourer
Jane, wife, 63

Cottage at Down Thomas
William Stare, Head of Family, 40, labourer
Sarah, wife, 39
Edwin, son, 16, app. shipwright
William, son, 15, attendant to masons
Richard, son, 11, scholar
Lizzie, daughter, 9, scholar
Mabel, daughter, 7, scholar
Rose, daughter, 4, scholar
George, son, 2
Ethel, daughter, 5 months

Cottage at Down Thomas
John Horn, Head of Family, 57, carpenter
Mary, wife, 56
William, son, 21, shipwright
Emma, daughter, 19
Samuel, son, 16, gardener
John Doddridge, grandson, 15
William Lee, 51, lodger

Cottage at Down Thomas
Elias Williams, Head of Family, 59, farm labourer
Elizabeth, wife, 53

Cottage at Down Thomas
Sampson Hammett, Head of Family, 50, farm labourer
Mary, wife, 45
William, son, 22, labourer
Charlotte, daughter, 14
Albert, son, 10, scholar
Emma, daughter, 7, scholar
Maud, daughter, 3

Cottage at Down Thomas
John Symons, widower, 49, smith
William, son, 19, shipwright
Emmanuel, son, 14, scholar
James, son, 11, scholar
Henry, son, 7, scholar
Margaret, sister, 50

Beers Farm
George Hammett, Head of Family, 45, agricultural labourer
Ann, wife, 43
George, son, 19
Alice, daughter, 9
Sydney, son, 4
Eva, daughter, 1

Beers Farm
Alexandra Dickenson, Head of Family, 35, labourer
Priscilla, wife, 35
Maria, daughter, 13, scholar
Ellen, daughter, 12, scholar
Thomas, son, 10, scholar

Beers Farm
John Algate, Head of Family, 29, agricultural labourer
Ann, wife, 39
Alfred, son, 1

Cottage at Down Thomas

St. Werburgh's Church Bells, 1909

Eleven bells were recast in this year at the expense of Mr. Richard Cory and converted into a ring of five. The inscriptions in the old bells were cast in the new ones, the whole work being undertaken by Aggetts of Chagford who also installed new fittings. The bowler hatted Mr. Aggett is on the right.

An Open Coach Outing to Totnes Races

The occasion is sometime in the 1920s and Iris Walke is here with her father Harold and mother Amy. Jimmy Milden, Edith and Charles Cawse, Jessie Avent, William Walke and Jack Holgate with his son Horace have been identified.

David Hammett, Head of Family, 54, farm labourer
Ann, wife, 52
David, son, 14
James, son, 11

Cottage at Down Thomas
William Bunker, Head of Family, 69, farm labourer
Jane, wife, 63
Albert Avery, nephew, 17, mason

Cottage at Down Thomas
Elizabeth Southern, widow, 61
Thomas, son, 25, ag. labourer
Elizabeth, daughter, 18
Joseph Algate, 93, father

Leaps Farm
James Milson, Head of Family, 65, farmer, 48 acres, 1 man
James, son, 31
John, son, 22
Elizabeth Hendy, granddaughter, 14, scholar

New Inn
William Allen, Head of Family, 37, innkeeper
Elizabeth, wife, 34
Alice, niece, 15, scholar
Mary Hendy, niece, 2

Taylors Farm, part
Elias Tolchard, Head of Family, 57, smith and wheelwright
Elizabeth, wife, 54

Taylors Farm, part
Thomas Gale, Head of Family, 29, mason
Charlotte, wife, 24

Cottage at Down Thomas
Robert Horn, Head of Family, 65, farm labourer
Elizabeth, daughter, tailoress
Edwin, son, 26, general labourer

Cottage at Down Thomas
James Hammett, Head of Family, 53, farm labourer
Maria, wife, 49
Ralph, son, 20
Mary, daughter, 14
James, son, 11
William, son, 9
Frances, daughter, 7
William Avery, 52, lodger, mason
Mary Avery, 45
Emily Smith, niece, 9, scholar

Princes Farm
John Stevens, Head of Family, 36, farmer, 130 acres, 2 labourers
Mary, wife, 37
John, son, 14, scholar
Louis, son, 12, scholar
Harold, son, 9, scholar
Percy, son, 5, scholar
Roscoe, son, 1
Mary Nilson, mother in law, 70, annuitant
Elizabeth, sister in law, 28, farm assistant

Cottage at Down Thomas
Joseph Dinner, Head of Family, 49, farm labourer
Maria, wife, 30
Frederick Axworthy, son, 10
George, son, 3
Edith, daughter, 2 months

Cottage at Down Thomas
George Axworthy, Head of Family, 66, labourer
Mary, wife, 68
Emma, daughter, 12

Cottage at Down Thomas
Charles Dingle, Head of Family, 74, farm labourer
Mary, wife, 71

Cottage at Down Thomas
Elizabeth(?) Horn, Head of Family, 38, gen. labourer
Ellen, wife, 37
Jane, daughter, 13
Henry, son, 11
William, son, 9, scholar
Ellen, daughter, 7

Cottage at Down Thomas
Samuel Avery, Head of Family, 54, mason
Jane, wife, 49
Nathaniel, son, 25, mason
James, son, 20, shipwright
Alice, daughter, 14, scholar
Samuel, son, 11, scholar
Maude, daughter, 5, scholar
Sarah, mother, 79

Princes Farm
Nicholas Lakeman, Head, 63, batchelor, farmer, 63 acres, 1 man, 1 boy
Ann Edwards, sister, 57, housekeeper
William Edwards, nephew, 19
Amelia, niece, 17
Henry Hammett, 15, servant

Langdon Barton
Thomas Pearce, Head of Family, 39, farmer, 500 acres, 9 men, 2 boys
Elizabeth, wife, 40
Sarah, daughter, 15
Emma, daughter, 4
Thomas, son, 12
John, son, 10
Sally Wills, 21, maid of all work
Grace Kelly, 18, maid of all work
William Dunn, 18, farm servant
Joseph Budge, 16, farm servant

Langdon Lodge
Christopher Cudlip, Head of Family, 52, gardener
Mary, daughter, 23
Caroline, daughter, 20

Boathouse
James Hockaday, Head of Family, 32, boatman
Harriett, wife, 33
Raymond, son, 1

Gabber Farm
Richard Williams, Head of Family, 55, farmer, 90 acres, 1 man
Elizabeth, wife, 45
Thomas, son, 20, farm servant
Andrew, son, farm servant
Ann, daughter, 11, scholar
Samuel, son, 4, scholar

Cottage Gabber
Emma Wilson, Head of Family, 35, washerwoman
Nora Smith, daughter, 8, scholar
Arthur, son, 6, scholar
Beatrice, daughter, 4, scholar
William, son, 2
Ethelbert, son, 1

Cottage Gabber
Edward W. Hendy, Head of Family, 40, carpenter
Jane, wife, 37
Edward, son, 16, gamekeeper
James, son, 11, scholar
Charlotte, daughter, 8, scholar
Frederick, son, 11 months
Ann Bryant, lodger, 81

Cottage Gabber
William Williams, Head of Family, 35, farmer's son
Mary, wife, 35
Florence, daughter, 9, scholar
William, son, 5, scholar
Adaline, daughter, 3

Heybrook Cottage
John Cook, Head of Family, 60, pensioner, Police force
Phillipa, wife, 55

Cottage Gabber
Maria Wilson, Head of Family, 74, widow
Edward, son, 46, labourer

Cottage Gabber
John Knott, Head of Family, 87, widower, labourer
Anne Baker, daughter, 61

Cottage Gabber
Sarah Sherwill, Head of Family, 65, widow
James West, son in law, 38, labourer
Louisa Parry, granddaughter, 10

Cottage Gabber
William Avery, Head of Family, 23, labourer
Kate, wife, 24
Blanche, daughter, 1
Blanche Owl, niece, 6

Langdon Farm Cottage
John Watts, Head of Family, 43, labourer
Mary, wife, 45
John, son, 20, farm labourer
George, son, 18, farm labourer
James, son, 17, farm labourer
Elizabeth, daughter, 15, pupil teacher
Carrie, daughter, 12, scholar

William, son, 9, scholar
Mary, daughter, 7, scholar
Ann, daughter, 1

Langdon Candry
Priscilla Trebble, Head of Family, 65, widow
M. C. Rendall, daughter, 26
Ada, daughter, 19
Thomas Rendall, son in law, 27, gardener

Langdon Cottage
Benjamin Samson, Head of Family, 29, gamekeeper
Jane, wife, 25
Donald, son, 1
Ida, daughter, 1 month

Josias Calmady Charity

This notice of 1884 makes interesting reading as Miss Laura Calmady refers to difficulties she has encountered in giving out each year her father's charity to the poor of Wembury. This declaration of finishing a fifty year practice is a sad reflection on those now distant years when local charities were fairly common.

THE CALMADY PENNY CLUB.

Miss LAURA CALMADY sends the Club tickets for this year, but is very sorry to tell the Members that these are the last, as the Club has now to be put an end to. Messrs. CORY and CANE as Churchwardens and Trustees of the Josias Calmady Charity have taken away from her all her own family money, a portion of which assisted her in keeping up this Club, as they say there are complaints all over the Parish about it, which she however does not believe. Messrs. CORY and CANE took away from her a part of the Family money soon after Mr. CORY came to Langdon; and allowed Mr. Adams to lay it out in Coals. They have now taken away the whole of the Calmady money from Miss LAURA CALMADY, which was left by her forefather, and amounts to £15 13s. 0d. a year—and by his will is specified to be laid out by the family, or by the Churchwardens, as is for the Poor of Wembury Parish. Miss LAURA CALMADY has received none of her family money since 31st December, 1883. She pays this year's Club, amounting to over £10 0s. 0d. herself, without any assistance from the Calmady Charity—which money, she hears, is now handed over to the Rev. C. BURGESS. She wishes every person in Wembury to understand the state of the case, and the reason of her breaking up the Club which has been carried on by her Family for nearly fifty years.

She truly hopes the Parishioners will see that the Poor of Wembury Parish will receive what is their due under the Will of her Ancestor, the directions of which her family have hitherto carried out, and have done so for two hundred y's.

Laura Calmady

Knighton,
Wembury,
31st December, 1884.

Gathering in Hay at Hollacombe about 1944

Mrs. Marjorie Rowland is serving tea to the group of men building a rick using a hay grabber. The hay had been forked by tractor to the foreground of this scene. Recalled here are Charlie Brooks, Bob Penwill, Ralph Avent, Arch Treleaven, Sam Gibson, Charlie Farmer (a Plymouth butcher) and Fred Rowland whose daughter Susan is also here.

Arthur L. Clamp – the man behind the books

Arthur Leslie Clamp was a man of boundless energy with a passion for helping others, particularly through his love of history. A printer by trade, he started his career in a printing company before moving his family from Exeter to Plymouth to teach at the Plymouth College of Art and Design, where he eventually became the Head of the Printing Department.

Arthur with his five children.

A Devoted Family Man

Despite his love of teaching, Arthur prioritised his family, always making it home by 5:30pm for tea. He and his wife, Rosemary, raised five children: Susan, Angela, Elizabeth, David, and Steven. Arthur would often combine his love of family and history by taking his children on Sunday walks, encouraging them to appreciate historical monuments by taking photos or making crayon rubbings of gravestones for his books. The family home at 203 Elburton Road was a hub of activity, with a large garden, featuring a two-storey fort and a makeshift swimming pool.

A Lifelong Learner and Adventurer

Arthur's thirst for knowledge extended beyond history to a deep curiosity about the world. He was passionate about exploring different cultures, traditions, and cuisines, often taking advantage of his long summer holidays as a teacher to travel to places like India, Russia, South America, the middle east and the USA, sometimes bringing one of his children along. This adventurous spirit even influenced his home life, as seen by the short-lived family tradition of steam-cooking vegetables after a trip to Iceland.

History is a prominent feature of family days out

Community and Philanthropic Spirit

His commitment to serving others was evident in his long-standing involvement with the Elburton Methodist Church. He was the Sunday School Superintendent for over 15 years and served as the editor of the wider church's monthly newsletter, "The Link," for a similar duration. After Rosemary's very sad passing, Arthur later remarried and, following a chance encounter with a professor from India, established a connection with a missionary school in Chennai. Together with his new wife, Christine, he co-founded a "Sponsor a Child's Education" program that continues to this day.

Pictured left – The cover of 'The Link' complete with hand drawn sketches of each church by Angela
Below right – Arthur Clamp promoting his latest book
Below left – Arthur at home with his first wife, Rosemary
Below centre – Arthur on holiday with his second wife, Christine

A Legacy of Learning and Positivity

Arthur's greatest passion was history, which he brought to life through tireless research, documentation, and the many books he authored. He was driven by a need to "never be stuck in a rut," constantly seeking new experiences, meeting new people, and expanding his knowledge. With a positive attitude and a great sense of humour, he was always ready to help others, leaving a lasting impact on his family and community. His children, Susan, Angela, Elizabeth, David, and Steven, remember him with love and gratitude.

David Clamp, 2025

A Legacy of Local History

Below is the story of how Arthur L Clamp began writing books, in his own words, drafted shortly before he passed away in 2001. I have only made minor alterations to this text, correcting grammatical errors that he did not survive to correct himself. When I first discovered this text, I was shocked to see my name mentioned. It seems that, unbeknownst to me, I shared my first PC with him. I suspect he used it during the day when I was at school, although I do have one memory of sitting with him and showing him how it worked. It has been a pleasure to pick up where he left off and see his books republished and redistributed, and to know that I was part of the story, even back then. It was also fascinating to discover that his pricing structure matches the way I have tried to price the books, with a third going to local sellers and the rest covering printing costs with a little left over for my expenses.

I am his eldest grandson, and it is a privilege to curate his legacy, which we are calling 'The Clamp Collection'. The very last line of the text originally reads "The following pages list all the titles." Sadly, that page is missing and we have no record of all the books he published and knowing that some of those were researched by other authors makes the process of finding them even harder. I look forward to one day completing the collection and seeing them all available again. And maybe, one day, I'll even start writing my own to add to the series. For now, here is his story in his own words.

Steven Gibson, 2025

Writing and Publishing Booklets on Local Topics and Areas

I started this interest in either 1968 or 1969 when living in Woodford. I had by these dates established the Department of Printing and I think I must have been looking for something different to do. The first titles were of A5 size proofed from type set at Clarke, Doble and Brendon, Ltd., Plymouth printers, and then made up into pages and printed at Sawtell and Neilson, Ltd., Totnes.

Then began a slow process of getting them out to shops, etc. which proved to be more time consuming and difficult than actually researching, writing and getting the books into print. However, I persisted and opened a business account with Barclays Bank on the Broadway. I was advised to give it a title so I called it "Westway Publications". There came along another problem, one of storage of paper and finished books which was solved when the family moved to Elburton in 1970.

I changed the printer to Penwell, Ltd., Callington, Cornwall, as he was then just setting up himself and his prices seemed very reasonable. I did not get any of the printers to make up the complete books. I hand folded the flat printed sheets, stitched the books on a small manual table stitcher and trimmed them in a small hand turned guillotine which I bought from someone in Penzance for £40. It was brought up in a van.

The trouble and time going to and fro to Callington was too much so I transferred the printing to PDS Printers, Prince Rock, Plymouth, and I have been with them ever since. Now they are at Plympton which is easy to reach and they fold the flat sheets which was turning out to be a long chore which only saved a small part of the printing costs.

All my first titles were written by myself. I took the photographs and developed them in the loft of the house, the type was set by now on a computer situated in the house at Elburton from which I had collected photographic lengths of text to cut up and law down as pages.

At some point I decided that I would do my own film processing of lith film so I bought a large second hand process camera from Kingsbridge and learnt through trial and error to make line negatives of the text and halftone negatives of the illustrations which proved more difficult than I anticipated. The main problem was trying to keep the developer in the large dish at the correct temperature as any change would affect the developing time. I replaced this old camera with a brand new one bought from Croydon, Surrey, costing £900. This has turned out to be a great asset cutting out an expensive part of the printer's costs and one crucial aspect of the work which I could control.

By the middle 1970s there were many outlets I had contacted in Plymouth, up to Dartmoor, Exeter, around to Torbay, Totnes, Dartmouth and the South Hams. The market for local books was much greater than I had first thought and through getting to know many local people undertaking research themselves had the chance to help and make up books for other people who had in most instances, got together a collection of photographs with some text in a rather muddled way. Through my experience in print I was able to shape up their work and get it into print and in every case I had to pay the printer and let the person have the royalties. In the majority of titles produced in this manner this was another way of producing titles and it did give some profit to my work. However, I must say that in a few cases I lost out by either the other person getting the numbers wrong, not returning any monies from stock I delivered or they thought that more of their books should have been sold.

The print run was usually 1,000 copies and from time to time I have had reprints of 250 copies. It took about ten years to clear the first print run so I always had large stocks in the garage, workshop, etc. The numbers sold during the early years was about 7,000 copies a year increasing to around 9,000 copies and for the whole of the enterprise about 500,000 have been sold. The booklets have become part of the local scene and many people collect them, shops regularly order copies and I go around certain areas month by month restocking or replacing titles as necessary.

During the past year or so I have started setting the text on a Packard Bell PC, something which I should have done some years back. I share it with Steven Gibson, my grandson. There appears to be no end to the market for local books, but I could not earn a regular income because of the long time it takes to sell stock.

However, now exceeding 100 titles made up mainly of A4 twenty-four page booklets, some folded guides, with selling prices set with a third going to the shop which is the trade custom, the original idea has been quite successful and could go on for ever.

Apart from monetary benefits, however spasmodically these might be, I have learnt a lot myself, met many interesting people and have become part of the local scene with requests to give talks and to advise people about getting into print.

Arthur L Clamp, 2001

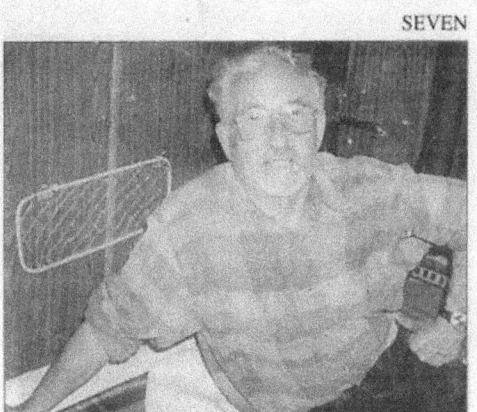

This newspaper article, published by the Evening Herald on 17th August 2001, forms a good record of his life. Just as he encourages us to learn more about local history, we encourage you to learn a little about him. For that reason, we have included these pages at the back of all the most recently republished books, in honour of his memory and recognition of his contribution to the community.